BLOOM'S
ReViews
COMPREHENSIVE RESEARCH & STUDY GUIDES

Herman Melville's
Moby-Dick

Edited & with
an Introduction
by Harold Bloom

First Printing
1 3 5 7 9 8 6 4 2

ISBN: 0-7910-4138-7

Chelsea House Publishers
1974 Sproul Road, Suite 400
P.O. Box 914
Broomall, PA 19008-0914

The Chelsea House World Wide Web site address is
http://www.chelseahouse.com

Contents

Editor's Note

My Introduction celebrates Captain Ahab as American Transcendentalist, more hero than villain, more Emersonian perhaps than Emerson himself was. Critical Views begin with the reviewer Evert Duyckinck, who grants Melville freshness of perception. D. H. Lawrence, novelist and seer, seems to read the novel from Moby-Dick's own perspective. With Lewis Mumford, we move to a judgment that exalts the book as a human defense against an indifferent or malign universe.

Shakespeare's large influence upon *Moby-Dick* is studied by W. E. Sedgwick, while Richard Chase regards Ahab as a Christ-like shaman. The extravagances of the novel's structure are seen as peculiarly American by Newton Arvin, after which Lawrance Thompson argues that a gnostic theology emerges from the book. R.W. B. Lewis traces the image of an Emersonian American Adam in *Moby-Dick*, while the comic aspects of Melville's narrative engross E. H. Rosenberry. The narrator's role is explored by Warner Berthoff, after which Paul Brodtkorb gives a brilliant exegesis of the color symbolism of whiteness in the novel, and Robert Zoellner contrasts the visions of Moby-Dick by which Ishmael and Ahab most differ. Humor and allegory respectively occupy Jane Mushabac and Bainard Cowan.

The politics of nineteenth century American expansionism are invoked by James Duban, while Frank Novak considers the aesthetics of terror in the book. Ishmael's role as survivor is W. B. Dillingham's focus, after which the context of slavery is seen by Robert K. Martin as crucial to *Moby-Dick*. In a remarkable reading, Leo Bersani finds a comprehensive image of America in the crew of the *Pequod*.

John B. Williams again brings Emerson, history, and Melville together, while John Bryant discovers an element of Shakespeare's Falstaff in Ahab, reminding us again how triumphantly comprehensive a figure Melville created for his prose epic's hero-villain.

Introduction

Ahab, the tragic protagonist of *Moby-Dick*, has only a few peers among American literary characters, and none of them is wholly of his eminence. Herman Melville risked overt allusions to a number of precursor figures in creating Ahab: Shakespeare's Macbeth and King Lear, Milton's Satan, Byron's Manfred and Cain, Shelley's Prometheus, and the Bible's Job. Most like Macbeth and Satan, Ahab is a hero-villain, conceived on a vast scale, cosmological as well as national. William Faulkner, who was profoundly influenced by *Moby-Dick*, said it was the book, above all others, that he himself wished he had written. To Faulkner, Ahab's end was "a sort of Golgotha of the heart become immutable as bronze in the sonority of its plunging ruin." And lest we misinterpret "ruin," Faulkner added: "[T]here's a death for a man, now."

Only Starbuck, his first mate, stands up against Ahab's quest, and all those who emphasize Ahab's villainy emulate Starbuck, except that Starbuck never fails to acknowledge Ahab's greatness. Starbuck remains loyal to his captain, while seeing that the hunt for Moby Dick is self-destructive and supposedly against God's purpose. But which God? Ahab, like Melville, has more than a Jobean dispute with God. Like Prometheus (and like Satan), Ahab is in rebellion against the sky-god. Melville, highly aware of the ancient Gnostic heresy, gives us an Ahab who has converted from Quaker Christianity to Parsee Manichaeism, and who staffs his personal whaleboat with a crew of Parsees (Persian Zoroastrians resident in India, to this day) headed by, as harpooner, the shadowy Fedallah. To a Gnostic, the god of this world is only an ignorant Demiurge, a false creator who is named as Yahweh or Jehovah in the Hebrew-Christian Bible, and whose representative is the Leviathan of the Book of Job. Melville names the Leviathan the White Whale or Moby Dick, who has maimed Captain Ahab, and whom Ahab, in turn, has vowed to destroy. In Gnostic terms, Moby Dick is the tyranny of demiurgical nature and time over the human, which retains however a spark of the true, unknown God, who dwells beyond the spheres, visible and invisible, of our cosmos. This spark is one with the flame that Ahab invokes in chapter 119, "The Candles":

> Oh! thou clear spirit of clear fire, whom on these seas I as Persian once did worship, till in the sacramental act so burned by thee, that to this hour I bear the scar; I now know thee, thou clear spirit, and I now know that thy right worship is defiance. To neither love nor reverence wilt thou be kind; and e'en for hate thou canst but kill; and all are killed. No fearless fool now fronts thee. I own thy speechless, placeless power; but to the last gasp of my earthquake life will dispute its unconditional, unintegral mastery in me. . . . Come in thy lowest form of love, and I will kneel and kiss thee; but at thy highest, come as mere supernal power; and though thou launchest navies of full-freighted worlds, there's that in here that still remains indifferent. Oh, thou clear spirit, of thy fire thou madest me, and like a true child of fire, I breathe it back to thee.

The right worship of fire, for Ahab, is to defy even it, in the name of one's own sacred selfhood, the spark within one. Ahab, at the close of chapter 132, "The Symphony," stares at the sea and is startled by observing "two reflected, fixed eyes in the water there," the eyes of his Parsee harpooner, Fedallah, but ambiguously his own eyes as well. The deep self, in Ahab, is an abyss, and contains a multitude of impulses, many of them antithetical to one another. Earlier in "The Symphony," Starbuck, speaking to himself, asks: "Is Ahab, Ahab?"

Ahab himself would have great difficulty with that question; *Moby-Dick* demonstrates the inadequacy of any answer. Melville had listened attentively to Ralph Waldo Emerson's New York City lectures, and was impressed, despite himself. Reading Emerson, Melville filled the margins with his dissents from our national sage, but the dissents were dialectical: More for better than for worse, Ahab is fiercely Emersonian. Melville's Shakespeare is the Emersonian Shakespeare of *Representative Men,* a book that reverberates throughout *Moby-Dick.* The very ocean itself in Melville's epic is Emersonian: It seethes with American selfhood, even as it forces limits upon American self-reliance. "Ask the fact for the form" Emerson advised, relying upon his ultimate, quite frightening formula: "Every natural fact is a symbol of some spiritual

fact." That is Captain Ahab's credo, and on its basis he interprets Moby Dick to symbolize a cosmically sanctioned evil in
the natural world. We tend to identify Melville with the narrator
Ishmael rather than with the tragic tyrant, the Macbeth-like and
Lear-like Ahab. I question the identification. It is true that
Ishmael survives, the only seaman from the *Pequod* who
remains to tell the story. Most critics have insisted that Melville
essentially disapproves of Ahab, but that, in my own judgment,
simply denies the experience of reading this sublime book. I
first read *Moby-Dick* in my childhood, and now at sixty-five I
do not sympathize with Ahab any less than I did then.
Americans in particular are attached to Ahab because his
authentic religion, which is neither Quaker nor Parsee, but an
eclectic Christian Gnosticism, is their own. Ahab personifies our
national sense of election, which doubtless does at least as
much harm as good, since it sends us forth on so many ruinous
quests. Though Ahab mesmerizes his crew, Ishmael included,
his spirit remains at once elitist and democratic. If the captain
of the *Pequod* sometimes seems Napoleonic (in the mode of
Emerson's Napoleon, in *Representative Men*), he also suggests
the heroic (and brutal) Andrew Jackson, idol of American
democrats (and Democrats, myself included). Jackson, an apos-
tle of slavery and a great murderer of Indians, rightly provokes
ambivalence among us now, but to Melville he was Old
Hickory, a prototype of Old Ahab, and the *Pequod* preserves
the spirit of Jacksonian democracy. Michael Paul Rogin, the
author of *Andrew Jackson and the Subjugation of the American
Indian* (1975), compares Ahab to Jackson because "Ahab
acquired authority over his white equals by appropriating the
power of people of color," presumably meaning his four harpooners in particular. But Ahab's Ahab—as Stubb the second
mate says: Ahab's authority—like Andrew Jackson's, is charis-
matic and royal. Like Lear, Ahab and Jackson are natural kings,
though, unlike Lear, they emerge from the people, as
Napoleon also emerged. But Ahab has a metaphysical
grandeur that breaks through his political matrix. Far more
even than the prophet Emerson, Ahab is the authentic
American Transcendentalist. All of us desire to strike through
the mask, but only Ahab realizes our desire. Walt Whitman
writes that the sunrise would kill him, if he could not, now and

always, send forth sunrise from himself. That is a benign Emersonianism, as dazzling and tremendous as the sunrise itself. Ahab cries out that he would strike the sun if it insulted him. That is a more savage Emersonianism, and may or may not be malign, but it also sets a new limit for American Transcendentalism. ❖

Biography of Herman Melville

Herman Melville was born in New York City on August 1, 1819, to Allan and Maria Gansevoort Melville. Both his grandfathers had served with distinction in the American Revolution, and his father headed a profitable import business. In 1830, however, financial troubles forced the family to move to Albany, and two years later Allan Melville died. After attending the Albany Academy, Herman Melville worked in a bank, on his uncle's farm, and in his brother's fur store. The family had to move once again, this time to the small town of Lansingburgh, outside of Albany, when the depression of 1837 bankrupted Melville's brother. For a short time, Melville taught at a country school and studied surveying in hopes of obtaining work on the Erie Canal building project.

To escape the bleak prospects at home, Melville joined the crew of a packet boat sailing for Liverpool, England, in 1839. Following another brief teaching stint, he left Fairhaven, Massachusetts, in January 1841 on the whaling ship *Acushnet*. A year and a half later, he and a friend acted on their boredom and discontent and deserted the ship at Nuku Hiva in the Marquesas Islands. He spent a few weeks with the Typee, who were rumored to be cannibals, before escaping on the whaling ship *Lucy Ann*. After being jailed in Tahiti for mutiny, he sailed to Honolulu, Hawaii. Finally, in August 1843, he joined the U.S. Navy to sail home on the frigate *United States* and was honorably discharged in Boston in October 1844.

Back home in Lansingburgh, Melville was encouraged by family and friends to write down his adventures. He read some books to expand his knowledge of the geography and ethnography of the South Seas and then composed *Typee*, an account of his time in the Marquesas Islands. The book, which was billed as nonfiction, was published in England and America in 1846. Its sequel, *Omoo*, debuted in 1847, and both volumes earned accolades from critics and the public.

Melville decided to pursue writing as a career and settled in New York City. In 1847, he married Elizabeth Shaw, the daughter of Massachusetts Supreme Court chief justice Lemuel Shaw, and soon started a family; the couple had two sons and two daughters. In 1849, he published *Mardi,* a sea story laden with allegory and symbolism, to great disappointment. Trying to regain his audience, Melville set aside his philosophical leanings to write the straightforward adventure tales *Redburn* (1849) and *White-Jacket* (1850). He drew upon memories of his first disheartening voyage to Liverpool to write the former and used his naval experience to depict life on a man-of-war in the latter.

After moving with his family to a farm near Pittsfield, Massachusetts, Melville once again concentrated on expressing himself fully. He developed a friendship with fellow author Nathaniel Hawthorne, who provided support while Melville undertook his most ambitious work, *Moby-Dick; or, The Whale.* Though the novel failed dismally upon its publication in 1851, it has since been heralded as a masterpiece of American literature. The story of Captain Ahab's obsessive quest to kill his cetacean nemesis, *Moby-Dick* blends a gripping adventure narrative, technical details of the whaling industry, and vivid characterizations with symbolism and deeply layered philosophical themes.

Although these were the most creatively productive years of his life, they may also have been the most difficult. The public rejection of *Moby-Dick* deeply depressed him. Struggling to support his wife and children on the farm, he had to borrow money from family members. To earn extra income, he wrote short stories for *Putnam's* and *Harper's* magazines. In 1852, he suffered another disappointment with the tragedy *Pierre,* an early psychological novel about a poet trying to be virtuous in the face of moral ambiguity. *Israel Potter* (1855), first serialized in *Putnam's,* concerned the apathetic treatment of a Revolutionary War veteran. His magazine pieces were collected in *The Piazza Tales* in 1856; they included "The Encantadas," about the Galapagos Islands, "Benito Cereno" (*Putnam's,* October 1855), about a slave ship rebellion, and "Bartleby the Scrivener" (*Putnam's,* November 1853), about a mysteriously recalcitrant clerk. In 1857, he published *The Confidence-Man,* a sardonic allegory on American manners.

Faced with the continued poor reception of his work, Melville gave up writing for a living. From 1856 to 1857, his father-in-law financed a trip to Europe and the Holy Land in the hope that it would alleviate his depression. Melville kept a diary of his journey, which was published in 1935 as *Journal Up the Straits,* and made the lecture circuit when he returned to the United States. In 1860, he embarked on his last sea voyage, sailing to San Francisco on a clipper ship owned by one of his brothers. Melville sold his farm in 1863 and returned to New York, where he worked as a customs inspector from 1866 until 1885.

During these years, he continued to write for pleasure. In 1866, he published his first volume of poetry, *Battle-Pieces and Aspects of the War,* which focused on the Civil War. *Clarel,* a long philosophical poem about a group of pilgrims in the Holy Land, followed in 1876. Two privately printed poetry collections, *John Marr and Other Sailors* and *Timoleon,* appeared toward the end of his life. Although his poetry has been dismissed by critics, the short novel he wrote sporadically between 1888 and 1891, *Billy Budd* (first published in 1924 in Volume 13 of the Standard Edition of his *Works*), has earned acclaim for its stirring depiction of arbitrary justice on a man-of-war.

Melville died in New York City on September 28, 1891. His death passed nearly unnoticed, and the brief obituaries marking it remembered *Typee* as his best book. However, Melville's work was rediscovered after World War I and has been receiving appreciative attention ever since. ❖

Thematic and Structural Analysis

Moby-Dick is a complex weave of adventure, fact, myth, superstition, history, and philosophy, narrated by the meditative wanderer Ishmael. Most prominent in the narrative is the adventure of the ship *Pequod,* led by Captain Ahab, who obsessively determines to destroy an infamous sperm whale known on the seas as the White Whale or Moby Dick, to whom he lost a leg on a previous voyage. The two other main components of the text are Ishmael's story of joining the *Pequod* and his extensive, interspersed discourse on whaling. So rich are the novel's symbols and themes that a summary seems almost blasphemous. In essence, Melville endeavored to explore humanity's place in the physical and metaphysical world in all its ambiguity and complexity. To do this he juxtaposed such ideas as Christian and pagan beliefs, civilization and savagery, science and superstition, gods and devils, free will and fate, the physical and the spiritual, and light and darkness.

The title of **chapter one,** "Loomings," sets a portentous mood. The narrator introduces himself with the famous line, "Call me Ishmael," the name of the outcast son of the biblical Abraham. He then begins the story of "some years ago" when, destitute in Manhattan, he decides to go to sea, a habitual antidote to his discontent. He—and all men, he maintains—are mystically attracted to the ocean because in it they see "the image of the ungraspable phantom of life." However, this time he goes to sea not as a merchant sailor but as a whaler. Drawn to the "wild and distant seas" and "perils of the whale," he initially believed he was motivated by his "own unbiased freewill and discriminating judgment," when in fact the Fates, he claims, were deluding him.

Beginning the novel's ominous pattern of poor luck, Ishmael arrives in New Bedford to find he has missed a boat to Nantucket (**chapter two**). He rejects two inns as expensive before deciding upon the third, The Spouter-Inn, whose landlord is named Peter Coffin. The number or sequence of three in *Moby-Dick* frequently has ominous significance.

Some of the novel's few comic moments take place during Ishmael's first night and morning at The Spouter-Inn (**chapters three to five**) and involve his acquaintance with the cannibal Queequeg. Because there are no unoccupied beds, Ishmael is told he can share a bed with a harpooner, who is out trying to sell his last New Zealand embalmed head. Ishmael reluctantly agrees. When the harpooner arrives, he does not notice Ishmael, who is already in bed. Ishmael observes him place the embalmed head in his bag, worship a black wooden idol at the fireplace, and smoke a pipe that resembles a tomahawk. Ishmael is most horrified by the skin of the "savage"—his whole body is purple and yellow and covered with tattoos, and his head is bald except for a knot of hair twisted on his forehead. When the harpooner springs into bed with a lit tomahawk, Ishmael cries out and they panic, having difficulty communicating because of Queequeg's broken English.

In **chapters six to twelve** Ishmael explores New Bedford, attends a Whalemen's Chapel Sunday service, and forms a "bosom" companionship with Queequeg. The chapel holds a congregation of "sailors, and sailors' wives and widows," who focus on memorial tablets of men who died at sea—some killed by whales. Realizing his potential fate, Ishmael raises several unanswerable questions about death. He then looks at what for him is the bright side of whaling. Losing his body at sea would free the better part of his being—his soul: "In fact take my body who will, take it I say, it is not me. And therefore three cheers for Nantucket; and come a stove boat and stove body when they will, for stave my soul, Jove himself cannot."

The old chaplain, a former harpooner named Father Mapple, mounts his pulpit, which resembles a ship's bow, and addresses the congregants. His sermon includes two lessons. He tells the story of the prophet Jonah, who, after being swallowed by a whale, "leaves all his deliverance to God" and achieves "true and faithful repentance; not clamorous for pardon, but grateful for punishment." He then says that because he, Mapple, is a greater sinner than the congregation, he therefore feels a greater responsibility not just to heed the lessons, but to preach "the Truth to the face of Falsehood." Though Mapple feels the burden of his position as a spiritual "pilot," his soul ultimately finds delight in acknowledging "no law or lord, but the Lord his God."

Back at The Spouter-Inn, Ishmael and Queequeg become close friends. With his simple, honest heart and brave spirit, Queequeg, and significantly not Father Mapple, seems to turn Ishmael's soul toward goodness: "No more my splintered heart and maddened hand were turned against the wolfish world. This soothing savage had redeemed it." In bed at night, Ishmael observes that "no man can ever feel his own identity aright except his eyes be closed; as if darkness were indeed the proper element of our essences, though light be more congenial to our clayey part." That is, man's spiritual identity, his soul, can be recognized only in darkness because light, a spiritual distraction, is but a tool for the inferior body to move about in the material world.

In **chapters thirteen to twenty-two** Ishmael and Queequeg journey to Nantucket to sign up with a whaler and board Ahab's ship. Aboard the *Moss,* which takes them from New Bedford, a young sailor who mimics Queequeg behind his back is swept overboard. Queequeg dives into the sea and rescues him, the first of three times in the novel Queequeg saves someone from drowning. In Nantucket, the two lodge at the Try Pots, over whose doorway hangs a topmast resembling a gallows. After Ishmael surveys three ships, he selects the third—the *Pequod*—a noble yet melancholy craft. Ishmael applies to two old former whale ship captains and investors in the *Pequod,* the Nantucket Quakers Bildad and Peleg, whose job it is to prepare the ship for voyage. After the Quakers argue over how much to pay Ishmael, they decide on a lower "lay" (percentage of the voyage's profits) than Ishmael had proposed, but he accepts their offer and promises to bring his harpooner friend Queequeg to meet them the next day. Prejudiced against the pagan, Peleg and Bildad first balk at hiring Queequeg. But after Ishmael declares that Queequeg is a member of the "whole worshipping world's" church, and after Queequeg impressively throws his harpoon, he is signed for a lay larger than Ishmael's. In the first of the novel's many prophecies and warnings, Peleg warns Ishmael about the forbidding ocean; describes the *Pequod's* captain, Ahab, as mysteriously "sick" since his leg was chewed by a whale; and tells him of the prophetical name given Ahab by his widowed, crazy mother, who saw in him a vile king, "grand, ungodly, god-like." Ishmael and Queequeg next meet a shabbily dressed, puzzling old sailor named Elijah, who, after learning that they have signed on with the *Pequod,* asks whether there was anything in the agreement about their souls. He then hints at Ahab's tormented history and the circumstances surrounding the loss of his leg. At dawn on the day they are to sail, they again meet Elijah, who asks if they saw some men heading toward the ship. Ishmael explains that "it was too dim to be sure." Elijah replies, "See if you can find 'em now," hinting at the deaths of sailors before them. The *Pequod* sails on Christmas Day.

Chapter twenty-three, "The Lee Shore," is a calm interlude before the stormy adventure. Ishmael sees Bulkington, a sailor he glimpsed at The Spouter-Inn, and launches into a meditation about land and sea. He concludes that while not facing life's unfathomable questions (symbolized by staying on land) may provide a feeling of safety, to do so is not to follow man's path to utmost spiritual potential—"in landlessness alone resides highest truth." Melville leaves unanswered, however, the questions of whether that truth is even attainable and whether the cost is too great.

In **chapters twenty-four to thirty-six**, the rest of the major characters are introduced, and Ahab's purpose to pursue Moby Dick—at any cost—is clearly established. Chief mate Starbuck is a careful Nantucket Quaker, a man of deep national reverence who kills whales only for the industrial products they provide. Because his father and brother were killed by whales, he is superstitious and trusts only those who fear them. Stubb, the second mate, is a jolly Cape Cod native whose fearless philosophy is that one should worry about danger and death when they come. Third mate Flask of Martha's Vineyard is dull and unconsciously fearless. Ahab, who finally appears on deck after a mysterious reclusiveness, is most marked by his grimness, his whale-jawbone leg, and a white streak on the right side of his otherwise scorched face. Starbuck's head harpooner is Queequeg; Stubb's is Tashtego, a Native American from Gay Head, Martha's Vineyard; Flask's is the imperial Daggoo, a black African. Dough-Boy the steward is instrumental in informing the crew of Ahab's Macbeth-like, nightmare-ridden sleeping habits. The Manxman is an old sepulchral man respected as having "preternatural powers of discernment." Tambourine-playing Pip, a young black shipkeeper, is hinted as destined to be among the angels.

Ahab spends his time gazing at the sea, steadying his whale-bone leg in specially made notches on deck. For a short time fair weather charms his mood, but he soon tosses his pipe—a symbol of serenity—overboard and is henceforth mostly seen pacing the deck or standing in the hatchway.

In these chapters Ishmael's intermittent whaling discourse first appears. He defends whaling as an honorable business that has furthered peace and democracy and bravely confronts the "terrors and wonders of God." In "Cetology" (**chapter thirty-two**) he endeavors to classify whales according to both his and other whalers' observations and the zoology of Melville's time.

In "The Quarter-Deck" (**chapter thirty-six**) Ahab reveals his design to exact vengeance upon the inscrutable supernatural forces that have insulted him, symbolized for him by the physical, natural being Moby Dick. Ahab nails a gold coin to the mast, promising it to the man who first spots the White Whale. This doubloon serves Ahab as a bright focus distracting the crew from his dark purpose—that is, to sacrifice all in his pursuit of Moby Dick—and as a tangible incentive to protect him from possible mutiny. He then conducts a dark ritual to further guarantee the crew's loyalty: The sailors drink from the harpoon sheaths of Ahab's three harpooner "cupbearers," and as he grips the crossed weapons of the mates and harpooners, all swear "[d]eath to Moby Dick. God hunt us all, if we do not hunt Moby Dick to his death!"

Chapters thirty-seven to forty-two present soliloquies by Ahab, Starbuck, and Stubb; information on Moby Dick; and explanations for the significance of his whiteness. Ahab sees his own soul as "damned in the midst of Paradise," too dark now to recognize beauty; Starbuck feels he must succumb to the plan of Ahab, whom he now hates and pities. Ishmael develops his vision of the whale. Among whalers, who perceive a malignant intelligence in the whale's boat-staving assaults, Moby Dick is considered the most perilous whale of the seas;

the more superstitious among them also believe he is ubiquitous and immortal. Despite many wounds (he is still stuck with
harpoons and a knife from Ahab), he lives on. He has a "snow-
white wrinkled forehead, and a high, pyramided white hump,"
and his body is of a streaked, spotted, marbled hue that leaves
a "milky-way wake of creamy foam, all spangled with golden
gleamings." Contrasting with this beauty is a "deformed lower
jaw" full of sharp teeth. Though Ahab had always felt the burden of this world's "intangible malignity," only after he lost his
leg did his "monomania" begin—did he project all evils upon
Moby Dick's hump and single-mindedly pursue the whale's
destruction.

The elusiveness of whiteness strikes panic in Ishmael's soul.
For every benign or sublime manifestation of the color (religious symbolism, bridal veils, the albatross) there is a malignant or dangerous one (ghosts, death shrouds, the great white
shark). But more than that, the whiteness of the Milky Way
suggests the "heartless voids and immensities of the universe"
and "stabs us from behind with the thought of annihilation."
And white light, which is the absence of color but is composed
of all colors, hints, Ishmael feels, at a world made up of everything but devoid of meaning. For Ishmael, the "Albino whale"
symbolizes all these meanings.

In **chapters forty-three to seventy-two** the first whale chases occur, three ships are encountered, and the character
Fedallah is introduced. One afternoon, while he and Queequeg
are weaving a mat to protect the ship's spars and rigging,
Ishmael perceives the weaving as a metaphor for his life. The
fixed threads of the warp represent necessity or fate; the shut-
tle, with which he weaves his own destiny into the "unalterable
threads," is Ishmael's free will; and the sword Queequeg uses
to push the woof, sometimes "slantingly, or crookedly, or
strongly, or weakly," is chance—which, Ishmael states, "has
the last featuring blow at events." Ishmael's meditations are
interrupted by Tashtego's wild cry announcing the voyage's
first whale sighting. Soon Ahab appears on deck surrounded by
"five dusky phantoms" headed by a tall, evil-looking man
whom Ahab calls Fedallah. Though a crewman had insisted he
heard strange sounds below deck one night, the appearance of
these men of "tiger-yellow complexion" comes as a surprise to

the sailors. Knowing that the *Pequod*'s owners would not like their crippled captain in dangerous boat chases, Ahab privately solicited this machinelike crew to man his whaleboat. Fedallah symbolizes the sleepless, ever-watchful, inhuman evil shadow of the soul Ahab has created in his darkness. Ishmael observes that Ahab's will "makes him a Prometheus; a vulture feeds upon that heart forever; that vulture the very creature he creates."

Before the first whale chase, Starbuck orders Ishmael in his boat because he senses a shared fear of whales. A storm approaches as they lower the boats. Queequeg harpoons a whale, but Starbuck's boat is swamped and the whale escapes. Separated from the *Pequod* by the storm, they spend the night alone on the sea and are nearly killed when at dawn the ship sails out of the mist and smashes into their boat.

One serene night some time later, Fedallah sees the silvery, celestial jet of a whale, which for nights is repeatedly seen and is believed to belong to Moby Dick.

When the *Pequod* encounters another Nantucket ship, the *Goney*, Ahab asks the captain, "Have ye seen the White Whale?" Unless for news of Moby Dick, Ahab never socializes with other captains. Soon a second homeward-bound Nantucket ship, the *Town-Ho*, is met and gives strong news of Moby Dick. However, we never hear this news. Instead, Ishmael recounts a story about this ship as he once told it to friends in Lima.

After a chase in which Stubb harpoons a whale, the whale experiences a gruesomely described death, and sharks feed on its fat. The whale is heaved up and "cut in," or stripped of its blubber, and the carcass floats out to sea. The whale's head, hanging alongside the ship before its values are extracted, is likened to the mythical Sphinx's. Ahab beseeches it to speak its secrets, as it has been where no living man has been before.

When the *Pequod* meets the ship *Jeraboam*, its captain, Mayhew, refuses any physical contact between the crews. Although there seem to be no symptoms, one of the *Jeraboam*'s crew, a fanatical Shaker and self-declared prophet who calls himself Gabriel, has convinced his shipmates that he cast an epidemic from a vial. While Mayhew, from a drop boat, tells the foreboding story of how his chief mate was killed by Moby Dick, Gabriel repeatedly shouts warnings against hunting the whale.

In these chapters, Ishmael's discourse on whaling becomes increasingly prominent. He claims landsmen do not understand the sperm whale's seemingly "deliberate designs of destruction to his pursuers." He tells us to erase from our minds popular depictions of whales, declaring that "the great Leviathan is that one creature in the world which must remain unpainted to the last." And to make the whale symbolically ubiquitous, he describes manifestations of it in art, industry, and nature. His statement "Long exile from Christendom and civilization inevitably restores a man to that condition in which God placed him . . . savagery" implies that the search for truth, symbolized by hunting the whale at sea, requires a departure from "civilized" spiritual assumptions.

In **chapters 73 to 105** the *Pequod* meets three more ships, Pip undergoes a transformation, and the symbolism of the try-works (a device that burns whale flesh to extract its oil) is presented. After Stubb and Flask kill a right whale, Stubb declares that Fedallah (also called the Parsee) is the "devil in disguise" and claims he stowed with Ahab to "get him to swap . . . his soul . . . and then he'll surrender Moby Dick." While Tashtego is engaged in the dangerous work of bailing out a sperm whale's "Heidelburgh Tun"—the part of the whale's head that contains pure spermaceti—he falls in and he and the head drop into the sea. Queequeg jumps in and pulls Tashtego from the head, for the second time saving a life.

The *Pequod* meets the German ship *Jungfrau* (Virgin), whose captain, Derick De Deer, asks for oil to feed his lamps. Lacking light, this ship's "virginity" is sad and empty (of fish and oil) rather than hopeful and wholesome. After receiving oil, the *Jungfrau* departs, and the two ships soon vie for the largest of eight whales suddenly descried. The *Pequod*'s superior harpooners strike first, and the crews kill the whale. However, the dead whale sinks—a rare occurrence—symbolizing the ultimate triumph of the awesome whale and portending the *Pequod*'s dismal future.

As Ahab continues his plan of sweeping through all sperm whale cruising grounds of the world, his isolation is reflected in his refusal to touch land along the way. Near Java Head, the *Pequod* chases a vast herd of sperm whales, and Malayan pirates briefly chase the *Pequod*. The boats are lowered and surrounded by the herd. Though the harpooners dart many whales, only one is captured and killed.

Soon the fragrantly named French ship *Bouton de Rose* (Rose-bud) is met in the midst of stinking dead whales over which fly a cloud of vultures. Its captain and crew are clad in devilish red velvet and red caps. Raising Ahab's frustration, this is the first ship encountered that has not seen Moby Dick.

A few days later, the tenderhearted Pip, who normally stays on board the ship when the boats are lowered, is pressed into service during a whale chase to replace an injured oarsman in Stubb's boat. After a whale is darted, Pip panics, jumps from the boat, and becomes entangled in a whale line, forcing the line to be cut and the whale to be lost. During the next chase, Pip again jumps overboard, but this time Stubb does not abandon the whale to rescue him, and Pip is only rescued by the *Pequod* after much time alone on the sea. The abandonment so traumatizes him that he loses his mind and believes he has seen God in the form of a great weaver. Ishmael sees wisdom in his rantings, suggesting that "man's insanity is heaven's sense."

Before the spermaceti from the whale Stubb killed can go to the tryworks, it is placed in tubs, where Ishmael and other crew members must squeeze the lumps it contains into fluid. While he is doing this, he feels cleansed of his oath against Moby Dick and suggests both the doom of the crew and their goodness. Inadvertently squeezing the hands of his fellow laborers, he looks affectionately into their eyes, seeing "long rows of angels in paradise, each with his hands in a jar of spermaceti."

This scene is quickly followed by the nighttime scene of the tryworks, whose odor Ishmael describes as "like the left wing of the day of judgment; it is an argument for the pit [hell]." As its flames rage, he observes that the *Pequod*, "freighted with savages, and laden with fire, and burning a corpse, and plunging into that blackness of darkness, seemed the material counterpart of her monomaniac commander's soul."

The *Pequod* meets the English ship *Samuel Enderby*, whose captain, Boomer, has an ivory limb in place of an arm lost to Moby Dick. Boomer has recently seen the White Whale but will not pursue Moby Dick again, saying, "[A]in't one limb enough?" As Ahab is leaving the *Enderby*, he splinters his leg and later has the carpenter make another. Ishmael then tells the story of a jolly experience he once had aboard the *Enderby*, ending the story with "This empties the decanter"—and hinting the end of comfort aboard the *Pequod*.

In **chapters 106 to 135**, the *Pequod* meets three final ships, encounters Moby Dick, and is destroyed. Oil is discovered in the *Pequod's* hold, but Ahab does not want to interrupt his pursuit of Moby Dick to locate and repair the leak. He and Starbuck have an argument over the matter that ends with Ahab pointing a musket at his first mate. But after Starbuck warns him to "beware of thyself," Ahab acts on a last shimmer of good conscience and orders the leak to be found.

After searching the dank hold, Queequeg becomes so ill that everyone gives him up for dead. Not wishing a typical sea burial, in which the body is wrapped in a hammock and dropped overboard, he requests that a canoe be made. But though he is pleased with the royally laden, canoelike coffin the carpenter fashions, he remembers an unfinished duty ashore, simply refuses to die, and quickly recovers.

In the Pacific, where Ahab expects to find Moby Dick, he has the blacksmith forge a special barb-ended harpoon—which Ahab tempers in the blood of his three pagan harpooners and baptizes in the name of the devil.

The day after the *Pequod* meets the homeward-bound ship *Bachelor*—which has encountered nothing but good luck—four whales are slain, one by Ahab. While Ahab's whaleboat is waiting to be picked up by the *Pequod*, his dark shadow the Parsee repeats three prophecies he has earlier made, that "neither hearse nor coffin" can be Ahab's; that Ahab will not die until he sees two hearses on the sea—the first "not made by mortal hands," the other made of American wood; and that before Ahab dies, Fedallah must go before him, as his "pilot," and though dead, must reappear to pilot Ahab to his death. From these seemingly impossible circumstances Ahab concludes that Fedallah has predicted he will "slay Moby Dick and survive it." And when Fedallah further predicts, "Hemp only can kill thee," Ahab erroneously interprets this to mean the gallows and derisively declares himself "immortal, then, on land and on sea."

In "The Candles" (**chapter 119**), the *Pequod* enters a storm and the narrative includes a climactic repetition of threes: The three tripointed masts are struck by lightning and catch fire; like a giant black cloud, Tashtego seems in the firelight three times his height; Stubb sees the burning masts as three good-luck spermaceti candles; lightning strikes again and the masts' flames leap to thrice their previous heights. Standing before the flames, Ahab speaks to the "clear spirit of clear fire,"—his "fiery father"—which as a younger man he had worshipped in the form of the life-giving sun but which he now associates with the destructive force of lightning and defies. When Starbuck tells him, "God is against thee" and beseeches him to take the ship home, Ahab satanically grabs his burning harpoon, threatens to impale anyone who tries to strike the sails, and blows out the harpoon's flame—the last fear of his heart.

Later Starbuck, "wrestling with an angel," decides not to murder Ahab, when he has the chance, with the same musket Ahab pointed at him. Soon Ahab senses a kindred soul in the mad Pip and adopts him, coming to "suck most wondrous philosophies" of "some unknown worlds" from the gentle ship-keeper. Each symbolically searches the other for the part of himself he has lost—Ahab his heart, Pip his courage. But because Ahab fears that Pip's good influence will cure him of his monomania, he locks Pip in his cabin.

One morning a man at the masthead falls and disappears into the sea, and the life buoy sinks after him. The lost life buoy is replaced by Queequeg's coffin, to which the carpenter attaches thirty separate life lines, one for each of the crew in case the *Pequod* sinks.

On a further note of loss, the *Pequod* meets the ship *Rachel*. Though its captain has encountered Moby Dick, he is searching not for the whale, but for a son lost at sea during the chase. Refusing to help in the search, Ahab says, "[M]ay I forgive myself. . . ."

The *Pequod* meets a last, miserable ship, the *Delight,* whose hollow-cheeked Nantucket captain reveals that the day before, Moby Dick killed five of his men, all but one of whom was buried by the sea. When the hammock-bound corpse of the fifth sailor is dropped overboard, the *Pequod* is sprinkled with its "ghostly baptism."

In a final calm interlude, a day's loveliness maternally caresses Ahab, who drops a last woeful tear into the sea. Revealing some of his history to Starbuck, he momentarily realizes the foolishness of his demonic solitude and laments the bitter unfairness of his leg. Symbolically bearing all the woes of humanity, he says, "I feel deadly faint, bowed, and humped, as though I were Adam, staggering beneath the piled centuries since Paradise." He looks into Starbuck's eyes for one last glimpse of home, questions what "remorseless emperor" has commanded his soul, then turns for Starbuck, who has left in despair after entreating Ahab's "noble soul" to flee homeward.

The last chapters comprise three chases of Moby Dick, who finally appears. On the first day, the whale bites Ahab's boat in half. On the second day, the boats are lowered (Ahab in a spare), and Moby Dick, after becoming entangled in harpoons, takes the boats of Stubb and Flask underwater, flips Ahab's boat and crew into the air, and flees. Although there are no fatalities, men are wounded, boats are damaged, Ahab's special harpoon is lost, and his leg is again splintered. After the crew is assembled on the *Pequod*'s deck, everyone realizes that the Parsee is missing and is perhaps dead—one of his prophecies fulfilled. Thinking of Moby Dick, Ahab declares that things that are drowning rise twice but the third time sink forever. But when the carpenter makes him a third leg, Ahab fails to realize the portentous symbolism.

On the third day, Ahab declares himself "nobler" than the "noble and heroic" unconquerable wind, against which the *Pequod* has been sailing. The boats are lowered, sharks follow only Ahab's boat, Starbuck envisions his fading past, and Moby Dick smashes Stubb's and Flask's boats with his tail. More of the Parsee's prophecies are fulfilled as his half-torn body is seen in a reel line wrapped around Moby Dick—the hearse not made by mortal hands. Ahab orders the crews of the damaged boats to return to the *Pequod,* leaving only his boat to fight the whale. Darted, Moby Dick tips the boat, and three oarsmen are tossed overboard. Two struggle back on board, but the third man cannot reach the boat. Moby Dick snaps the line and proceeds to attack the *Pequod,* biting its prow. As the ship begins to sink, the crew say their last prayers. Ahab recognizes the *Pequod* as another of Fedallah's prophecies—the man-made hearse of American wood that cannot be his. His cry—"Oh, lonely death on lonely life! Oh, now I feel my topmost greatness lies in my topmost grief . . . let me then tow to pieces, while still chasing thee, though tied to thee, thou damned whale!"—is the antithesis of Father Mapple's delight through faith in the one Christian God, making him the tragic but spiritually unconquered hero of grief. Ahab darts Moby Dick for the last time, the line (the hemp Fedallah said alone could kill him) catches him around the neck, and he is dragged underwater. The vortex created by the sinking *Pequod* sucks Ahab's whaleboat and its crew under, and everything is shrouded by the ancient sea.

In the **epilogue**, Ishmael describes how he alone survived. He explains that the Fates ordained him to replace Ahab's bowman, who had replaced the Parsee. When the three oarsman are flung from Ahab's whaleboat, Ishmael is the one who cannot get back on board and thus witnesses the ensuing destruction from a safe distance. Queequeg's former coffin rises from the sunken *Pequod* (Queequeg for the third time saving a life), and Ishmael clings to it for a whole day, surrounded by inexplicably harmless sharks, before being rescued by the ship *Rachel.* However, the *Rachel* is ever woefully searching, and Ishmael, significantly commenting on his identity, says she "only found another orphan." ❖

—*Amy Connelly*

List of Characters

Ishmael is the open-minded, bravely curious, meditative narrator of *Moby-Dick*. He reveals little about his origins and serves mainly as an observer to the novel's action. Impatient with civilized society, indifferent toward organized religion, he finds in the sea a soul-satisfying pantheism. Nevertheless, he comes to recognize the darker side of nature.

Ahab is the old, embittered captain of the *Pequod*. After losing a leg to the whale Moby Dick on a previous voyage, he begins a monomaniacal quest to exact revenge on what he regards as the unjust forces that control the universe, embodied for him in the White Whale. He puts all his intelligence, all his cunning—indeed, the entire crew he commands—into the service of this dark endeavor. Although Ahab at times seems to recognize the madness of his course, he defiantly follows it to its tragic end.

Father Mapple, a former harpooner, is chaplain of the Whalemen's Chapel in New Bedford, where Ishmael hears him preach. His role as God's pilot of souls embodies the Christian ideal of service. Acknowledging no law or lord but the Christian God, he believes, will bring the soul delight—a view that is diametrically opposed to Ahab's dark vision.

Queequeg, Starbuck's harpooner and Ishmael's friend, is a tattoo-covered South Seas cannibal of royal blood. Brave and benevolent—he twice risks his life to save someone from drowning—Queequeg challenges conventional notions of civilization and savagery.

Starbuck, the *Pequod*'s chief mate, is a careful, conscientious, good-hearted man. Though he is devoutly religious, his is a faith that avoids confronting potentially troubling questions. He recognizes that Ahab's quest will likely end in disaster, but he lacks the will to oppose the captain.

Stubb, the jolly, profane second mate, enjoys the adventure of whale hunting without fearing death. He fancies himself wise but is actually quite unreflective.

Flask, the third mate, is a spiritually and intellectually obtuse man whose fearlessness stems from his lack of imagination.

Fedallah (also called the Parsee) is a tall, evil-looking man whom Ahab secretly engages to lead his private whale-chasing crew. He makes several prophecies about Ahab's fate and is the symbolic shadow that Ahab's dark soul has created.

Pip is a small, fearful black shipkeeper who is forced to replace an oarsman in Stubb's whaleboat. After he jumps from the boat in panic during a whale chase, he is temporarily abandoned at sea, loses his mind, and becomes obsessed with his cowardice. In his madness, however, he makes prescient observations and is symbolically adopted by Ahab as the goodness his own soul has lost.

Tashtego, Stubb's fierce harpooner, is an American Indian from Gay Head, Martha's Vineyard.

Daggoo, Flask's harpooner, is a huge, strong pagan from Africa.

Peleg and *Bildad,* investors in the *Pequod,* are Nantucket Quakers and former whale ship captains who hire Ishmael and Queequeg.

Elijah is a shabbily dressed old sailor who makes puzzling, foreboding prophecies about Ahab and the voyage to Ishmael and Queequeg before they board the *Pequod.* ❖

Critical Views

[Evert A. Duyckinck (1816–1878) was a noted American editor and literary critic. He compiled a *Portrait Gallery of Eminent American Men and Women of Europe and America* (1873) and coauthored the important *Cyclopaedia of American Literature* (1856). In this extract from a review of *Moby-Dick* from the *Literary World* (which he edited), Duyckinck presents a mixed but on the whole favorable view of the work, in contrast to many other reviewers who found *Moby-Dick* obscure and long-winded.]

A difficulty in the estimate of this, in common with one or two other of Mr. Melville's books, occurs from the double character under which they present themselves. In one light they are romantic fictions, in another statements of absolute fact. When to this is added that the romance is made a vehicle of opinion and satire through a more or less opaque allegorical veil, as particularly in the latter half of Mardi, and to some extent in this present volume, the critical difficulty is considerably thickened. It becomes quite impossible to submit such books to a distinct classification as fact, fiction, or essay. Something of a parallel may be found in Jean Paul's German tales, with an admixture of Southey's Doctor. Under these combined influences of personal observation, actual fidelity to local truthfulness in description, a taste for reading and sentiment, a fondness for fanciful analogies, near and remote, a rash daring in speculation, reckless at times of taste and propriety, again refined and eloquent, this volume of Moby Dick may be pronounced a most remarkable sea-dish—an intellectual chowder of romance, philosophy, natural history, fine writing, good feeling, bad sayings—but over which, in spite of all uncertainties, and in spite of the author himself, predominates his keen perceptive faculties, exhibited in vivid narration. ⟨. . .⟩

The intense Captain Ahab is too long drawn out; something more of *him* might, we think, be left to the reader's imagination. The value of this kind of writing can only be through the personal consciousness of the reader, what he brings to the book; and all this is sufficiently evoked by a dramatic trait or suggestion. If we had as much of Hamlet or Macbeth as Mr. Melville gives us of Ahab, we should be tired even of their sublime company. Yet Captain Ahab is a striking conception, firmly planted on the wild deck of the Pequod—a dark disturbed soul arraying itself with every ingenuity of material resources for a conflict at once natural and supernatural in his eye, with the most dangerous extant physical monster of the earth, embodying, in strongly drawn lines of mental association, the vaster moral evil of the world. The pursuit of the White Whale thus interweaves with the literal perils of the fishery—a problem of fate and destiny—to the tragic solution of which Ahab hurries, amidst the wild stage scenery of the ocean. To this end the motley crew, the air, the sky, the sea, its inhabitants are idealized throughout. It is a noble and praiseworthy conception; and though our sympathies may not always accord with the train of thought, we would caution the reader against a light or hasty condemnation of this part of the work.

⟨. . .⟩ we acknowledge the acuteness of observation, the freshness of perception, with which the author brings home to us from the deep, "things unattempted yet in prose or rhyme," the weird influences of his ocean scenes, the salient imagination which connects them with the past and distant, the world of books and the life of experience—certain prevalent traits of many sentiment. These are strong powers with which Mr. Melville wrestles in this book. It would be a great glory to subdue them to the highest uses of fiction. It is still a great honor, among the crowd of successful mediocrities which throng our publishers' counters, and know nothing of the divine impulses, to be in the company of these nobler spirits on any terms.

—Evert A. Duyckinck, [Review of *Moby Dick*], *Literary World*, 22 November 1851, pp. 403–4

D. H. Lawrence on Hunting Moby Dick

[D. H. Lawrence (1885–1930), the celebrated British novelist and poet, was also an astute if idiosyncratic critic. Among his critical works are *Movements in European History* (1921) and *Fantasia of the Unconscious* (1922). In this extract—a variant version of the chapter on Melville from his celebrated treatise, *Studies in Classic American Literature* (1923)—Lawrence examines the symbolism of the hunting motif in *Moby-Dick*.]

Herman Melville's biggest book is *Moby Dick*, or *The White Whale*. It is the story of the last hunt. The last hunt, the last conquest—what is it?

American art symbolises the destruction, decomposition, mechanizing of the fallen degrees of consciousness. Franklin and Crevecoeur show the mechanizing of the shallowest instincts and passions, appetites; Cooper and Melville the deeper worship-through-contumely of the fallen sexual or sacral consciousness; Poe the direct decomposition of this consciousness; and Dana and Melville the final hunting of the same consciousness into the very Matter, the very watery material, last home of its existence, and its extinction there. Remains the entry into the last state, and into fulness, freedom.

St. John said, "there shall be no more sea." That was esoteric. Exoterically, Dana and Melville say the same. The Sea, the great Waters, is the material home of the deep sacral-sexual consciousness. To the very depths of this home Melville pursues the native consciousness in himself, and destroys it there. When he has really destroyed this sacral-sexual consciousness, destroyed or over-thrown it, then John's prophecy will be fulfilled. There will be no more sea.

Moby Dick is the story of this last symbolic hunt. Moby Dick is a great white whale, the Leviathan of the waters. He is old, hoary, monstrous and snow-white; unspeakably terrible in his wrath; having been repeatedly attacked, he swims now alone in the great, pathless seas.

He is the last warm-blooded tenant of the waters, the greatest and the last. He is the deep, free sacral consciousness in man. He must be subdued.

In himself he is warm-blooded, even lovable. But he must be conquered. Curious are his counterparts in the world. The whole of the South Pacific seems to worship, in hate, the shark or the crocodile, the great cold-blooded tenants, lords of the water, fiendish and destructive lords. Curious how shark and crocodile patterns, with grinning teeth, dominate aboriginal decoration-designs in those regions. The same crocodile worship is found in Africa, very wide-spread. In China, however, the dragon, the Leviathan is the dragon of the sun: as the Mantis, surely another dragon of the sun, dominates the Bushmen. Is not this that inordinately ancient relic of the pre-Flood worship, a relic from that era when the upper consciousness was the anathema, and the glory and the triumph was all in the sensual understanding, incomprehensible to us now?

Melville writes in the peculiar lurid, glamorous style which is natural to the great Americans. It gives us at first a sense of spuriousness. To some it merely seems wordy and meaningless, unreal. It comes, I think, from the violence native to the American Continent, where force is more powerful than consciousness, and so is never gracefully expressed. The life-force itself is so strong that it tends to come forth lurid and clumsy, obscure also. It causes also a savage desire to go to extremes, to hasten to extremes, whether of idealism or of violent action.

So, in beginning *Moby Dick*, we must be prepared for the curious lurid style, almost spurious, almost journalism, and yet *not* spurious: on the verge of falsity, still real. The book starts off with a semi-metaphysical effusion about water, and about the author's attraction to this element; it goes on with some clumsy humorisms, till it arrives in the sea-town of New Bedford. Then actual experience begins. It is curiously like cold material record, touched-up into journalese: neither veritable nor created. One cannot help feeling that the author is pretentious, and an amateur, wordy and shoddy. Yet something glimmers through all this: a glimmer of genuine reality. Not a reality of real, open-air experience. Yet it is a reality of what takes place in the dark cellars of a man's soul, what the psychoanalysts call the unconscious. There is the old double set of values: the ostensible Melville, a sort of Emersonian transcendentalist, and the underneath Melville, a sort of strange underworld, under-sea Yankee creature looking with curious, lurid vision on the upper world. It is the incongruous mixture of ideal heaven and the uncouth incoherence of a self-conscious adolescent. The reality comes from the adolescent, the uncouth, unformed creature, not from the idealist.

It is no use pretending that Melville writes like a straightforward, whole human being. He is hardly a human being at all. He gives events in the light of their extreme reality: mechanical, material, a semi-incoherent dream-rendering. What the futurists have tried to do, Dana and Melville have pretty well succeeded in doing for them. These two are masters of the sheer movement of substance in its own paths, free from all human postulation or control. The result is nearly like artifice, a sort of rank journalism. But we must restrain a too hasty judgment. The author is never quite himself. He is always at the mercy of the rank, the self-conscious idealism which still rules white America, he always has to handle artificial values.

Melville tries to square himself with the intellectual world by dragging in deliberate transcendentalism, deliberate symbols and "deeper meanings." All this is insufferably clumsy and in clownish bad taste: self-conscious and amateurish to a degree, the worst side of American behavior. When however he forgets all audience, and renders us his sheer apprehension of the world, he is wonderful, his book commands a stillness in the soul, an awe.

> —D. H. Lawrence, "Herman Melville's *Moby Dick*" (1923), *The Symbolic Meaning: The Uncollected Versions of* Studies in Classic American Literature, ed. Armin Arnold (New York: Viking Press, 1964), pp. 213–15

LEWIS MUMFORD ON THE MEANING OF *MOBY-DICK*

[Lewis Mumford (1895–1990) was one of the leading intellectuals of the twentieth century. He was

renowned for his studies of urban life and human conduct in such works as *The Conduct of Life* (1951), *The
Transformations of Man* (1956), and *The City in History*
(1961). In this extract from his monograph on
Melville—a landmark in the restoration of Melville's
reputation—Mumford finds the fundamental meaning
of *Moby-Dick* to be a depiction of humanity's heroic
struggle against a hostile universe.]

But *Moby-Dick*, admirable as it is as a narrative of maritime
adventure, is far more than that: it is, fundamentally, a parable
on the mystery of evil and the accidental malice of the universe. The white whale stands for the brute energies of existence, blind, fatal, overpowering, while Ahab is the spirit of
man, small and feeble, but purposive, that pits its puniness
against this might, and its purpose against the blank senseless-
ness of power. The evil arises with the good: the white whale
grows up among the milder whales which are caught and cut
up and used: one hunts for the one—for a happy marriage,
livelihood, offspring, social companionship, and cheer—and
suddenly heaving its white bulk out of the calm sea, one comes
upon the other: illness, accident, treachery, jealousy, vengeful-
ness, dull frustration. The South Sea savage did not know of the
white whale: at least, like death, it played but a casual part in
his consciousness. It is different with the European: his life is a
torment of white whales: the Jobs, the Aeschyluses, the
Dantes, the Shakespeares, pursue him and grapple with him, as
Ahab pursues his antagonist.

All our lesser literature, all our tales of Avalon or Heaven or
ultimate redemption, or, in a later day, the Future, is an evasion
of the white whale: it is a quest of that boyish beginning which
we call a happy ending. But the old Norse myth told that
Asgard itself would be consumed at last, and the very gods
would be destroyed: the white whale is the symbol of that per-
sistent force of destruction, that meaningless force, which now
figures as the outpouring of a volcano or the atmospheric dis-
ruption of a tornado or again as the mere aimless dissipation of
unused energy into an unavailable void—that spectacle which
so disheartened the learned Henry Adams. The whole tale of
the West, in mind and action, in the philosophy and art of the
Greeks, in the organization and technique of the Romans, in

the precise skills and unceasing spiritual quests of the modern man, is a tale of this effort to combat the whale—to ward off his blows, to counteract his aimless thrusts, to create a purpose that will offset the empty malice of Moby-Dick. Without such a purpose, without the belief in such a purpose, life is neither bearable nor significant: unless one is polarized by these central human energies and aims, one tends to become absorbed in Moby-Dick himself, and, becoming a part of his being, can only maim, slay, butcher, like the shark or the white whale or Alexander or Napoleon. If there is no God, exclaims Dostoyevsky's hero, then we may commit murder: and in the sense that God represents the totality of human purpose and meaning the conclusion is inevitable.

It is useless to derive man's purposes from those of the external universe; he is a figure in the web of life. Except for such kindness and loyalty as the creatures man has domesticated show, there is, as far as one can now see, no concern except in man himself over the ceaseless motions and accidents that take place in nature. Love and chance, said Charles Peirce, rule the universe: but the love is man's love, and although in the very concept of chance, as both Peirce and Captain Ahab declare, there is some rough notion of fair play, of fifty-fifty, of an even break, that is small immediate consolation for the creature that may lose not the game, but his life, by an unlucky throw of the dice. Ahab has more humanity than the gods he defies: indeed, he has more power, because he is conscious of the power he wields, and applies it deliberately, whereas Moby-Dick's power only seems deliberate because it cuts across the directed aims of Ahab himself. And in one sense, Ahab achieves victory: he vanquishes in himself that which would retreat from Moby-Dick and acquiesce in his insensate energies and his brutal sway. His end is tragic: evil engulfs him. But in battling against evil, with power instead of love, Ahab himself, in A. E.'s phrase, becomes the image of the thing he hates: he has lost his humanity in the very act of vindicating it. By physical defiance, by physical combat, Ahab cannot rout and capture Moby-Dick: the odds are against him; and if his defiance is noble, his methods are ill chosen. Growth, cultivation, order, art—these are the proper means by which man displaces accident and subdues the vacant external powers in the universe: the way of growth is not to become more power-ful but to become more human. Here is a hard lesson to learn: it is easier to wage war than to conquer in oneself the tendency to be partial, vindictive, and unjust: it is easier to demolish one's enemy than to pit oneself against him in an intellectual combat which will disclose one's weaknesses and provinciali-ties. And that evil Ahab seeks to strike is the sum of one's ene-mies. He does not bow down to it and accept it: therein lies his heroism and virtue: but he fights it with its own weapons and therein lies his madness. All the things that Ahab despises when he is about to attack the whale, the love and loyalty of Pip, the memory of his wife and child, the sextant of science, the inner sense of calm, which makes all external struggle futile, are the very things that would redeem him and make him victorious.

Man's ultimate defence against the Universe, against evil and accident and malice, is not by fictitious resolution of these things into an Absolute which justifies them and utilizes them for its own ends: this is specious comfort, and Voltaire's answer to Leibniz in Candide seems to me a final one. Man's defence lies within himself, not within the narrow, isolated ego, which may be overwhelmed, but in that self which we share with our fellows and which assures us that, whatever happens to our own carcasses and hides, good men will remain, to carry on the work, to foster and protect the things we have recognized as excellent. To make that self more solid, one must advance positive science, produce formative ideas, and embody ideal forms in which all men may, to a greater or less degree, partic-ipate: in short, one must create a realm which is independent of the hostile forces in the universe—and cannot be lightly shaken by their onslaught. Melville's method, that of writing *Moby-Dick,* was correct: as correct as Ahab's method, taken lit-erally, that of fighting Moby-Dick, was fallacious. In *Moby-Dick,* Melville conquered the white whale in his own consciousness: instead of blankness there was significance, instead of aimless energy there was purpose, and instead of random living there was Life. The universe *is* inscrutable, unfathomable, malicious, *so*—like the white whale and his element. Art in the broad sense of all humanizing effort is man's answer to this condition: for it is the means by which he circumvents or postpones his doom, and bravely meets his tragic destiny. Not tame and gen-

tle bliss, but disaster, heroically encountered, is man's true
happy ending.

—Lewis Mumford, *Herman Melville* (New York: Literary Guild
of America, 1929), pp. 184–87

WILLIAM ELLERY SEDGWICK ON SHAKESPEARE'S INFLUENCE ON MELVILLE

[William Ellery Sedgwick (1899–1942) is the author of
the posthumously published *Herman Melville: The
Tragedy of Mind* (1945), from which the following
extract is taken. Here, Sedgwick explores the influence
of Shakespeare on the shaping of the tragic framework
of *Moby-Dick*.]

The influence of Shakespeare on Melville was fundamentally a
profound and pervasive act of fertilization. There are many indi-
cations of this that one can point to, some of them important
and others superficial. That is, there are numerous and diverse
parallels in language, in emotional effect, in situation and tragic
action between *Moby Dick* on the one hand, and, on the other,
King Lear, Hamlet, Macbeth, Othello and *Timon.* I must repeat
what I quoted in the last chapter from Melville's remarks on
Shakespeare: "those deep faraway things in him; those occa-
sional flashings-forth of the intuitive Truth in him; those short,
quick probings at the very axis of reality;—these are the things
that make Shakespeare, Shakespeare." Now look at *Moby Dick.*
"Oh God!" cries Ahab, "Oh God! that man should be a thing for
immortal souls to sieve through!" There is Ahab's angry retort
to the ship's carpenter, "Thou art as unprincipled as the gods,
and as much of a jack-of-all-trades." And I might add any number of other instances where Melville, following Shakespeare,
put in the mouths of his own "dark" characters words which
probe jaggedly at the very axis of reality.

A point of difference must come up first which is high-light-
ed by the many similarities between them. This difference
might have been expected from the peculiarity of Melville's

response to Shakespeare, his response to him primarily as a seer or truthteller. This was Melville's first criterion in estimating a poet's worth. How independent and rigorous he was in applying the criterion of truthfulness can be seen in his letter to Evert Duyckinck of March, 1849, in which he wrote, "Now I hold it a verity, that even Shakespeare, was not a frank man to the uttermost." Shakespeare, he granted, was handicapped by the prejudices of his time when all men were forced to wear a muzzle on their souls. Thereupon Melville added, with an optimism which his own experience was to belie, "but the Declaration of Independence makes a difference."

In *Moby Dick,* as in Shakespeare's tragedies, there is a solid, crowded foreground of material things and of human characters and actions. Yet this solid ground will suddenly seem to give under our feet, so that we feel ourselves hung momentarily over the abyss. We owe this sensation to the fact that solidity has been sacrificed to transparency for the sake of a more immediate view into the ultimate. Shakespeare was satisfied to leave the mysterious background of life to random probings or to inference. Melville could not. He was bound by many diverse considerations—by his inherited and his temperamental Calvinism, by the American pioneer in him as well as the Puritan—to confront the truth as directly and comprehensively as possible. In *Moby Dick* the mysterious background truth looms in the foreground of palpable facts. It articulates itself in those facts and by doing so it confers upon them something of an apocalyptic scale and intensity foreign to Shakespeare's prevailing naturalism.

> —William Ellery Sedgwick, *Herman Melville: The Tragedy of Mind* (Cambridge, MA: Harvard University Press, 1945), pp. 85–86

RICHARD CHASE ON AHAB

[Richard Chase (1914–1962) was a prominent American literary critic and the author of *Quest for Myth* (1949), *Walt Whitman Reconsidered* (1955), and

The American Novel and Its Tradition (1957). In this extract from his book on Melville, Chase examines the character of Ahab, finding him both a prototypical American of his time as well as a symbolic shaman and Christ-figure.]

I should say that Ahab is as much the American of his time as was Homer's Odysseus the Greek of his time or Joyce's Leopold Bloom the Jew of his time. He is the American cultural image: the captain of industry and of his soul; the exploiter of nature who severs his own attachment to nature and exploits himself out of existence; the good progressive American; the master of the most beautifully contrived machine of his time; the builder of new worlds whose ultimate spiritual superficiality drives him first to assume an uneasy kingship and a blind, destructive motive of revenge, and then gradually reduces him to a pure, abstract fury on whose inhuman power he rides off into eternity, leaving nothing behind but disaster for the races of the world and an ambiguous memory of the American flair which accompanied the disaster and was the only hint of moral meaning or of solace for the future or for the dead at the bottom of the Pacific. This much, and much more, of the epic hero of *Moby-Dick* was given to Melville by the folk tales and legends of New England and the frontier. But Melville was not Homer, not having Homer's rich mythical material. He had to generate much of the myth as he went along; he had to exploit foreign mythologies and to adduce and re-create the very folk tales he was at the time transmuting into epic. Thus Melville constructs Ahab out of many myths and many men.

Ahab is a primitive magician who tries to coerce man and the universe by compulsive ritual; and again like the magicians, he insults and castigates his god. He is the *shaman,* that is, the religious leader (common among certain tribes of American Indians) who cuts himself off from society to undergo his private ordeal, through which he attains some of the knowledge and power of the gods. The *shaman* is usually deeply neurotic and sometimes epileptic—the savior with the neurosis. Again, Ahab is the culture hero (though a false one) who kills the monsters, making man's life possible.

But Ahab also resembles an even more momentous mythical being: Christ. Were he not so committed to his "monomaniac" pursuit of the whale, Ahab might have been the source of genial spirits and reviving life. He is "stricken" and "blasted," says Captain Peleg, but "Ahab has his humanities." And in the beautiful chapter called "The Symphony," Ahab, overcome for a moment by the insinuating feminine vitalities of the Pacific air, is seen to shed a tear into the sea, a tear of compassion for the suffering in the universe. "Nor did all the Pacific contain such wealth," Melville says, "as that one wee drop." The memory of the true Savior remains, though obscurely, in Ahab's personality; he works out his fated failure within the ghostly scaffolding of the Savior's career on earth. Like the Savior, Ahab is preceded by a prophet; namely, the demented Elijah, who so persistently importunes Ishmael and Queequeg with his divinations shortly before the *Pequod* sets sail. Indeed, Ahab speaks of *himself* as a prophet. "Now then," he says, addressing himself, "be the prophet and the fulfiller one." Again, we are told that Ahab sleeps "with clenched hands, and wakes with his own bloody nails in his palms." The pun is unavoidable. But there is this difference between Ahab and Christ: these are Ahab's own nails. He is not a sacrifice; he is a suicide.

In his poem on Melville, W. H. Auden says of Ahab that "the rare ambiguous monster . . . had maimed his sex." And indeed the fall of the year—some time, that is, before Christmas, when the *Pequod* sailed—Ahab, like the divine hero Adonis, suffered a "seemingly inexplicable, unimaginable casualty." He was found lying on the ground, "his ivory limb having been so violently displaced that it had stakewise smitten him and all but pierced his groin." Like the savior-heroes, Ahab withdrew from the world after being wounded. Only when the *Pequod* left Nantucket behind and began to feel the springlike breath of the south did Ahab return to the world to perform his fated task. Like a resurrected savior he stepped from his cabin, in which he had been "invisibly enshrined," a "supreme lord" in his "sacred retreat." The ordeal Ahab suffered in his spiritual transit of withdrawal and return left him a transfigured being. When he came on deck, "as if, when the ship had sailed from home, nothing but the dead wintry bleakness of the sea had . . . kept him so secluded," his appearance absolutely appalled Ishmael, who had been watching the afterdecks for some time with "foreboding shivers." As Ahab finally stood at the taffrail on his "barbaric white leg," he looked "like a man cut away from the stake, when the fire has overrunningly wasted all the limbs without consuming them, or taking away one particle of their compacted aged robustness." Ahab stood before the crew, says Melville, "with a crucifixion in his face; in all the nameless regal overbearing dignity of some mighty woe." Ahab was in appearance, if not in reality, the Savior. For apparently he had returned to mankind from his ordeal, having acquired the new insight, the new sense of dedication, the new sanctity necessary for the accomplishment of his task.

—Richard Chase, *Herman Melville: A Critical Study* (New York: Macmillan, 1949), pp. 43–45

NEWTON ARVIN ON THE STRUCTURAL DIFFICULTIES OF *MOBY-DICK*

[Newton Arvin (1900–1963) was a notable American critic. Among his works are *Hawthorne* (1929), *Whitman* (1938), and *Longfellow: His Life and Work* (1962). In this extract from his book on Melville, which won a National Book Award, Arvin explores the difficult structure of *Moby-Dick,* which, he argues, could only have been written by an American.]

To speak of the structure and the texture of *Moby Dick* is to embark upon a series of paradoxes that are soberly truthful and precise. Few books of its dimensions have owed so much to books that have preceded them, and few have owed so little; not many imaginative works have so strong and strict a unity, and not many are composed of such various and even discordant materials; few great novels have been comparably concrete, factual, and prosaic, and few of course have been so large and comprehensive in their generality, so poetic both in their surface fabric and in their central nature. In form alone *Moby Dick* is unique in its period, and that too in a sense more special than the sense in which every fully achieved work of literature is unique. Such a book could only have been written by an American, and an American of Melville's generation, working as he did in a kind of isolation from the central current of European writing in his time—an isolation quite consistent with his keeping abreast of it intellectually—and, while losing something in consequence, gaining something indispensable he could not otherwise have had.

Given his kind of creative power, Melville was wholly fortunate in his literary derivations and development. As we have seen, his springboard had never been the English or European novel, not at any rate in its great characteristic mode, the mode of the social novel, the novel of manners, the novel of "real life." He belonged to a society that was in some of its aspects too archaic to find a natural place for forms so advanced as these, in his own origins, as if he belonged to the Bronze Age or at least to the Age of Migrations, were partly in oral storytelling, the story-telling of sailors and travelers, and partly in forms that were either subliterary or at the best on a modestly and hesitantly literary level. He had begun as a writer of reportorial travel books, books that were simply further examples of the "journal" or "narrative," and in a certain sense he continued to be such a writer in *Moby Dick*. It is wholly natural that Owen Chase's *Narrative* should have been so vital to him, and that one pole of *Moby Dick* should be constituted by the informative chapters on whales and whaling. Melville's need as an artist was to take the small, prosy, and terribly circumscribed form he had inherited, and somehow make it a vehicle capable of bearing a great imaginative weight, of expressing great visionary theme. His problem was to find the bridge between J. Ross Browne and Camoëns. He had quite failed to find it in *Mardi;* he had run away from his true matter in pursuit of an allegorical will-o'-the-wisp, and the result had been fiasco. A better wisdom had come to him in consequence; a better sense of his own right path. His own right path was, as Emerson would say, to "ask the fact for the form": to remain faithful to his own crass, coarse, unideal, and yet grandiose material—the life of American whalers—and to make of its unpromising images his symbols, of its hardly malleable substance his myth.

It is what he does in *Moby Dick*. There is no question here of chimerical priests and maidens, of symbolic blooms and allegorical isles and Spenserian bowers; no question of symbols wilfully imposed upon the meaning from without; no question of what Melville himself now calls "a hideous and intolerable allegory." In their stead one finds a fable almost bare in its simplicity and, on the surface, journalistic in its realism; the fable of a whaling vessel that sets out from Nantucket and, like some actual whaling vessels, comes to a disastrous end on the cruising-grounds near the Line. This tale is launched in pages so homely in their substance, despite their intensity of expression, that its earliest readers might almost have doubted whether they had to do with a "novel" or only with another and rather more dashing "narrative." It comes to a close in pages in which we are still encountering men like the bereaved Captain Gardiner and the vessels like the *Rachel* of Nantucket. The skipper and the mates of the *Pequod* hail from Nantucket or the Cape or the Vineyard; all the characters, including the pagan harpooners, and even perhaps the Parsees, are such men as might have been found, though some of them rarely, on an actual whaler of the 'forties. In their company we sail over well-known whaling routes, past familiar capes and headlands, giving chase not to fabulous monsters but to Sperm Whales and Right Whales of the sort that men had taken by the thousands, and having glimpses as we do so of other creatures—sharks, squid, swordfish, seahawks—such as Owen and Cuvier had classified. In short, with one or two great exceptions, the substance of *Moby Dick* is as faithful to sober fact as that of Owen Chase's or Ross Browne's book; if the impress on the imagination is that of a high poetic form it is not because the poetry is "allegorically" imposed on the stuff, but because the stuff is allowed to render up its own poetic essences.

It does so partly because the organizing structure of the fable—the Voyage, with its clear beginning and its predestined catastrophe—is at once so firm and simple and so large and free in its elasticity: like the structure of the *Odyssey* or the *Lusiads,* it is both strict and pliable. It is a fable, moreover, which, though it took shape in the most natural way out of a set of dense facts and tough, unromantic conditions, could nevertheless be made concrete and dramatic through a group of basic, primary symbols (the sea, the quest, the great "fish," the ship, the watery tomb) and of incidental or secondary symbols (the sword-mat, the monkey-rope, the sharks, and others) that are both immediate and primordial, both local and archetypal, both journalistic and mythopoeic. They are, moreover, at the same time wonderfully various and powerfully interrelated, so that the balance, as Coleridge would say, between "sameness" and "difference" is all but perfect. In any composition less completely integrated there might seem to be a hopeless incongruity between Ahab's pipe and the mystic Spirit-Spout, as between the jolly, unimaginative Stubb and the Satanic Fedallah: in the setting of *Moby Dick* they are no more incongruous than, in the *Odyssey,* the swine of Eumaeus and the magic veil that Ino bestows on Odysseus.

> —Newton Arvin, *Herman Melville* (New York: William Sloane Associates, 1950), pp. 151–54

LAWRANCE THOMPSON ON THE THEOLOGY OF *MOBY-DICK*

[Lawrance Thompson (1906–1973) taught at Columbia and Princeton, where he was the Holmes Professor of Belles Lettres. Among his books are *Young Longfellow* (1939), *William Faulkner: An Introduction and Interpretation* (1963), and a three-volume biography of Robert Frost (1966–76). In this extract from his celebrated study, *Melville's Quarrel with God* (1952), Thompson maintains that the underlying theological message of *Moby-Dick* is the belief that the world is the product of a malevolent God.]

There is considerable proof that Melville's own mind had become hypnotized by his own belief in Ahab's ultimate action as an ideal of action, because that kind of action translated death into anti-Christian victory, even as Byron suggested in the last line of his poem *Prometheus.* In *Mardi,* Melville had said, "So, if after all these fearful, fainting trances, the verdict be, the golden haven was not gained;—yet, in bold quest thereof, better to sink in boundless deeps, than float on vulgar shoals; and give me, ye gods, an utter wreck, if wreck I do." In *White-Jacket,* he had said, "Nature has not implanted any power in man that was not meant to be exercised at times. . . . The privilege, inborn and inalienable, that every man has, of dying himself, and inflicting death upon another, was not given us without a purpose. These are the last resources of an insulted and unendurable existence." In the Bulkington chapter of *Moby-Dick,* as we have seen, he said, ". . . so better is it to perish in that howling infinite, than be ingloriously dashed upon the lee, even if that were safety! For worm-like, then, oh! who would craven crawl to land! Terrors of the terrible! is all this agony so vain? Take heart, take heart, O Bulkington! Bear thee grimly, demi-god! Up from the spray of thy ocean-perishing—straight up, leaps thy apotheosis!" In *Pierre,* his description of his autobiographical hero echoes all three of these passages:

"Now he began to feel that in him, the thews of a Titan were forestallingly cut by the scissors of Fate. He felt as a moose, hamstrung. All things that think, or move, or lie still, seemed as created to mock and torment him. He seemed gifted with lofti-ness, merely that it might be dragged down to the mud. Still, the profound willfulness in him would not give up. Against the breaking heart, and the bursting head; against all the dismal lassitude, and deathful faintness and sleeplessness, and whirlingness and craziness, still he like a demi-god bore up. His soul's ship foresaw the inevitable rocks, but still resolved to sail on, and make a courageous wreck."

The ideal, in each of those passages, is the ideal of the "cour-ageous wreck." But Pierre's final boldness of posture bears a strikingly close resemblance to Ahab's, particularly when Pierre says, near the end of his life, "Now, 'tis merely hell in both worlds. Well, be it hell. I will mold a trumpet of the flames, and, with my breath of flame, breathe back my defiance!"

Shades of Teufelsdrockh's "Everlasting No" and shades of the Satan School of literature to which Melville belonged! He was temperamentally and artistically inclined to strike the Byronic pose and rebaptize himself, not in the name of the Father, but in the name of Satan. Even if we are forced to see in Melville's sophomoric attitude a certain indication of arrested development, it is better to recognize him for what he was than to inflate his attitude into something which it was not.

Baldly stated, then, Melville's underlying theme in *Moby-Dick* correlates the notions that the world was put together wrong and that God is to blame; that God in his infinite malice asserts a sovereign tyranny over man and that most men are seduced into the mistaken view that this divine tyranny is benevolent and therefore acceptable; but that the freethinking and enlightened and heroic man will assert the rights of man and will rebel against God's tyranny by defying God in thought, word, deed, even in the face of God's ultimate indignity, death.

Happily, the greatness of a work does not depend entirely on what it says, even though this seems to me to be the ultimately controlling factor. Once we have come to understand the complexities of style and structure and symbol in *Moby-Dick*, we are able to admire anew the brilliance of Melville's success in achieving a highly intricate artistic correlation, which actually rests on the symbolic extensions of a single word, "Leviathan."

—Lawrance Thompson, *Melville's Quarrel with God* (Princeton: Princeton University Press, 1952), pp. 241–43

R. W. B. LEWIS ON THE AMERICAN HERO IN *MOBY-DICK*

[R. W. B. Lewis (b. 1917) is a distinguished American critic and biographer. He has written *The Poetry of Hart Crane* (1967), *Edith Wharton: A Biography* (1975), and other volumes. In this extract, Lewis traces the use of a particularly American type of hero, which he calls the American Adam, in the "Try-Works" chapter of *Moby-Dick*.]

Only so much of Melville and his writing is relevant here as bears upon the history of the American Adam: as symbol of a possible individual condition, as type of hero for fiction. But it is the nature of Melville's achievement that any fragment of his writing, or all of it together, can seem to respond directly to any serious question we ask of it. Any set of symbols, as Mark Van Doren gracefully remarked about *The Tempest,* "lights up as in an electric field" when moved close to a novel or *novella* of Herman Melville. The best of him corresponds to the "substances" mentioned in *White-Jacket,* which "without undergoing any mutations in themselves, utterly change their colour, according to the light thrown upon them." Critical light, pumped out all too dazzlingly these later years, has thus been able to disclose a multitude of Melvilles: the God-hating Melville, the father-seeking and castration-fearing Melville, the traditionalist-and-quasi-Catholic Melville; Melville the cabalistic grubber in obscure philosophies, Melville the liberal democrat and defender of the vital center, and Melville the jaunty journalist of the adventures of boys at sea. Such proliferating multisidedness is an evidence of genius, but not, in my opinion, of the very highest genius; and if there are already more Melvilles than there have ever been Dantes, it is partly because Dante's poetry is firm in an inner coherence and is not totally plastic to the critic. But a certain lack of finish was a deliberate element in Melville's aesthetic as well as his metaphysic; and criticism can always finish the story according to its private enthusiasms. With this *caveat,* we may consider Melville the myth-maker at work upon the matter of Adam.

We may begin with a passage from chapter 96 in *Moby-Dick,* "The Try-Works"—taking the passage as a summary of Melville's attitude to innocence and evil; as an example of Melville's way with the material (attitudes, tropes, language) available to him; and as a guide for the rest of this chapter.

The incident of "The Try-Works" will be recalled. Ishmael falls asleep at the tiller one midnight, as the "Pequod" is passing through the Java seas heading northward toward the haunts of the great sperm whales. Waking up, but not yet aware that he has been asleep, Ishmael finds himself staring into the mouth of hell: "a jet gloom, now and then made ghastly by flashes of redness," an infernal scene through which giant shadow-shapes like devils are moving about some dreadful work. He is "horribly conscious of something fatally wrong"; "a stark bewildered feeling as of death" comes over him. Then he realizes— just in time to swing about, grasp the tiller, and save the ship from capsizing—that he has turned in his sleep and is facing the two furnaces, or "try-pots," amidships, and the three black harpooners stoking the masses of whale blubber from which the oil is extracted ("tryed-out"). ⟨. . .⟩

Melville, that is to say, had penetrated beyond both innocence and despair to some glimmering of a moral order which might explain and order them both, though his vision remained slender, as of that moment, and the center of light not yet known, but only believed in—and still ambiguously, at that. But, like the elder Henry James, Melville had moved toward moral insight as far as he had just because he had begun to look at experience dramatically. He had begun to discover its plot; and Melville understood the nature of plot, plot in general, better than anyone else in his generation. For Melville was a poet.

So "alternative" is a misleading word, in speaking of any characteristic passage in Melville. Indeed, one way to grasp this passage and Melville's achievement in general is to notice that Melville is *not* posing static alternatives but tracing a rhythmic progression in experience and matching the rhythm as best he can in language. This is the way of a Platonist, and not of a polemicist; much more, it is the way of a poet. We still tend, for all the good criticism of our time, to read a poem the way we watch a tennis-match: turning our heads and minds back and forth between what we presume to be unchanging opponents, as though a poem moved between fixed choices of attitude before plumping conclusively for one of them as the unequivocal winner. The best kind of poem is a process of generation—in which one attitude or metaphor, subjected to intense pressure, gives symbolic birth to the next, which reveals the color of its origin even as it gives way in turn by "dying into" its successor. Such a poem does not deal with dichotomies but in live sequences.

Here, then, in "The Try-Works," we have a series of displacements. Artificial light gives way to natural light, darkness to morning, and the imperative to the indicative. Then dawn and sunlight yield to darkness, to the moon and "the dark side of the earth"—to hell, to sickness, and to death. But hell and death are the source at last of a new and loftier life, new "sunny spaces" and new imperatives. Those sunny spaces are not the same bright skies of the opening stanza. The moral imagination which contemplates the sunny spaces in stanza 3 has been radically affected by the vision of hell and death at mid-point. The sunny spaces (tragic optimism) relate to the earlier morning skies (empty-headed cheerfulness) as does the Catskill eagle to "the other birds upon the plain"; it is the sky, as the eagle is a bird—but bird and sky have been raised to a higher power.

—R. W. B. Lewis, "Melville: The Apotheosis of Adam," *The American Adam: Innocence, Tragedy and Tradition in the Nineteenth Century* (Chicago: University of Chicago Press, 1955), pp. 130–31, 133–34

EDWARD H. ROSENBERRY ON COMEDY IN *MOBY-DICK*

[Edward H. Rosenberry, formerly a professor of English at the University of Delaware, is the author of *Melville* (1979) and *Melville and the Comic Spirit* (1955), from which the following extract is taken. Here, Rosenberry discusses the various forms of comedy employed by Melville in *Moby-Dick*.]

The face of *Moby-Dick*'s comedy is of course its jocular-hedonic aspect. It is the lightest of the book's ingredients and by virtue of that fact provides the buoyancy it needs to keep its ponderous cargo afloat. On the surface *Moby-Dick* sparkles with the rakish laughter of *Omoo*.

In the person of Ishmael, Melville once again portrayed himself "in flight from the deadly virtues." Like Long Ghost, Ishmael is frank to "abominate all honourable respectable toils," and is troubled with an impish itch to tweak the nose of authority. He is a sociable sort of fellow whose sense of humor is admirably unimpaired when the joke turns out to be on him.

> However, a good laugh is a mighty good thing, and rather too scarce a good thing; the more's the pity. So, if any one man, in his own proper person, afford stuff for a good joke to

anybody, let him not be backward, but let him cheerfully allow himself to spend and be spent in that way. And the man that has anything bountifully laughable about him, be sure there is more in that man than you perhaps think for.

By no means all that is in Ishmael is brought out by the simple laughter he provokes; yet from the beginning he spends himself freely for pure amusement and thus firmly establishes himself as a vital and sympathetic character.

He introduces himself with typical Yankee self-ridicule, setting his erstwhile dignity as a schoolmaster and aristocrat in ludicrous contrast to his current forecastle status. In the opening action of the story he blossoms into a full-fledged Yankee sucker, not so callow as Redburn, but as comically green in the face of perilous contingencies. The laconic trickster to whom Ishmael plays goat is Peter Coffin, landlord of the Spouter-Inn at New Bedford. As much a stranger to whaling as young Redburn was to the sea at large, Ishmael is easily sold on the idea of sharing a bed with a "dark complexioned" harpooner and only gradually succumbs to certain vague apprehensions, to the mounting amusement of the landlord—and the reader. The scene in which Peter Coffin hoodwinks him about the peddling of Queequeg's "head" is not a subtle one, but it is constructed with a sure professional touch. The compounded misunderstanding and the exaggerated alternation of furious and icily restrained reactions are devices as old and as new as farce itself. For the landlord the fun does not end until far into the night, when, still grinning happily, he is called by a frantic Ishmael to intercede with the tomahawk-wielding savage who has just leaped into bed with him. The reader, remaining with poor Ishmael in the interim, is in addition privy to all the comic alarms that Peter Coffin can only imagine—alarms that rapidly progress from mere nervous imaginings to a succession of hair-raising realities as Queequeg reveals his barbaric person and his more barbaric religious rites to the stunned Presbyterian in the bed. Such scenes, Weaver has written, "are, for finished humour, among the most competent in the language."

Once Queequeg has revealed the gentleness beneath his horrific exterior, Ishmael ceases to be Peter Coffin's goat and turns to a bit of "skylarking" of his own. In the Try-Pots Inn at Nantucket he rallies the distracted Mrs. Hussey about her menu, promotes a second helping by uttering "the word 'cod' with great emphasis" through the kitchen door, and gulls his savage companion about the presence of a live eel in his soup. When, later, the devout owners of the *Pequod* refuse to sign on Queequeg unless he has been converted, Ishmael presents his tattooed friend as a deacon in the "First Congregational Church" and outfaces their indignant skepticism with a pious lecture on the brotherhood of man.

As parties to Ishmael's sportiveness, all of these lesser characters have, like Peter Coffin, comic qualities to match. Mrs. Hussey emerges from her negligible role with startling memorability. She runs her establishment with forthright masculinity, simplifying her bill of fare for all three meals to two kinds of chowder ("Clam or cod?") and depriving Queequeg of his inseparable harpoon as a precaution against suicide on her premises. When she discovers the harpoon missing in the course of Queequeg's day-long fast and meditation behind locked doors, her practical and humanitarian concerns war in her with a ludicrous alternation ("there goes another counterpane—God pity his poor mother!—it will be the ruin of my house"), and she crisply orders a sign made to eliminate the two principal banes of her professional existence: "No suicides permitted here, and no smoking in the parlor."

—Edward H. Rosenberry, *Melville and the Comic Spirit*
(Cambridge, MA: Harvard University Press, 1955), pp. 93–95

WARNER BERTHOFF ON MELVILLE'S NARRATORS

[Warner Berthoff (b. 1925) is a retired professor of English at Harvard University. He is the author of *Edmund Wilson* (1968) and *Hart Crane: A Reintroduction* (1989). In this extract from *The Example of Melville* (1962), Berthoff studies the function of the narrator in Melville's works, specifically *Moby-Dick*.]

The Melvillean narrator acts and is acted upon, being a character in his own recital. (Indeed in the five books before *Moby-*

Dick there are scarcely any other developed characters; there are only sketches, types, more or less distinctive examples of the conditions of life being described.) But more especially he *tells*—recalls, considers, meditates, emphasizes, explains. He acts, that is, primarily in his formal role, coming to life through his own narrative voice. A certain degree of absorbed passivity and reflective detachment marks off the Melvillean narrator from the Romantic hero of passion and energy or from the type of the quester after experience. His character, as recording witness, is to remain radically open to experience without being radically changed by it; he is to identify and judge matters without equivocation, yet not show himself too overridingly anxious to impose his outlook upon them. In this respect the part he plays goes according to the arch-Romantic conception of the poet or artist—the conception of the creative intelligence as the agent of a "negative capability," the source of whose power is in the free and sympathetic readiness of its responses to the phenomena of life. Thus, the role given the narrator in Melville's chronicles is determined, we may say, not only by the situation and actions being rendered but by the very job of rendering them. Certainly Melville used his narrators to convey his own thought and feeling; what should be emphasized is that he was at the same time subjecting his reckless personal bent toward declamatory self-expression to the formal discipline of a naturally suitable working method.

This reserved freedom of response in Melville's narrators, and the corresponding rhythm of their absorption and detachment, is what sets them apart as moral agents in his fiction. They are not made to claim any greater power over their lives' conditions than is granted any one else. The intuition that "to treat of human actions is to deal wholly with second causes" applies to them as well. Yet there is a difference, which shows first in the simple mechanics of the first-person mode as Melville used it. Though the narrator will speak of his own behavior deterministically and see himself at any given moment fate-dogged and nearly powerless, the very fact that he is not only describing the events of the narrative from another point in time but taking just as much time as he needs and wants in order to recall them makes for a certain actual freedom from them and equanimity about them. The business of retrospective narration presumes, and creates, its own detachment, its own independence, its own (as we like to say of Ishmael and his admirable breed) "survival." So Ishmael's qualities—his unflagging readiness, bluff stoicism, impartial mockery, sensuous sympathy, and intellectual vivacity, all maintained in the face of the most fearful omens, and strongly counterpointing Ahab's madness—do not make their impression on us in the book as a dramatic model and triumph of exemplary character. What they do directly refer us to is just that art of which they are the means and the first effects, the convention-rooted art by which the book as we have it has been created. The rare congeniality of the narrator (i.e., of his voice) marks, formally, the creative fulfillment of the narrative genre Melville had steadily been working in, and is the first sign of his mastery in *Moby-Dick*.

Melville had an impressive flair, as a writer, for direct, unmediated assertion, but when he attempted to make it the whole basis and instrument of his exposition, as in *Pierre*, it could go outrageously to waste. In *Moby-Dick*, on the other hand, the plain procedures of narrative recollection, the tangible gathering up of past events into the present sequences of a recital, are the means, practically, of his success; through them the most prodigious and terrific phenomena are subdued to the masterable logic of human time and human understanding. All other characters in the book exist only within the action of the story, and are wholly subject, as we see them, to its course of happenings. The narrator, however, exists to tell the whole story out, and therefore moves above it and around it, as well as through it, in relative freedom. The result is that the leading gestures of the work as a whole, and the pattern of the experience displayed in it, are never quite the same as what its staged events add up to—or would add up to if presented dramatically only. At least a double focus is established; we see things as they are in the immediate passion of human effort, but also as they appear to detached observation in the mere succession of their occurrence.

—Warner Berthoff, *The Example of Melville* (Princeton: Princeton University Press, 1962), pp. 120–22

PAUL BRODTKORB ON MELVILLE'S USE OF THE COLOR WHITE
IN *MOBY-DICK*

[Paul Brodtkorb is the coeditor of *Interpretations of American Literature* (1959) and the author of *Ishmael's White World* (1965), from which the following extract is taken. Here, Brodtkorb explores the significance of Melville's use of the color white in *Moby-Dick*.]

Ishmael's reasoning on the subject of whiteness is characteristically dialectical and circular, because such mental motion is descriptively most appropriate to his ambiance.

His dialectical analysis begins with a statement of the most common associations of whiteness, a color that may call to mind beauty, aristocracy, joy, innocence, benignity, honor, justice, divinity, spotlessness—"whatever," in short, "is sweet, and honorable, and sublime"; yet, "there . . . lurks an elusive something in the innermost idea of this hue, which strikes . . . panic to the soul." Whiteness is polarized in this way because, when "coupled with any object terrible in itself," it heightens "that terror to the furthest bounds." For example, "the irresponsible ferociousness" of the white bear "stands invested in the fleece of celestial innocence and love; and hence, by bringing together two such opposite emotions in our minds," frightens us "with so unnatural a contrast." It is as if the contradictory emotions evoked by the dialectical movement within the mind cancel each other out, leaving nothing, and therefore dread. Yet to assert this makes whiteness only one half responsible for the dread, and this is clearly not so: self-canceling emotional opposition is insufficient to account for the terror of the white bear, for "were it not for the whiteness, you would not have that intensified terror." There must be something inherent in whiteness itself; and the fact that creatures not in themselves ferocious or terrible—an albatross, "the White Steed of the Prairies," a human Albino—can evoke "spiritual wonderment and pale dread," "trembling reverence and awe," repellence and shock; this fact is evidence that the final source of emotional ambiguity is to be found in the color itself.

Nature herself assumes the power of whiteness to intensify dread when "in her least palpable but not the less malicious agencies" she enlists "among her forces this crowning attribute of the terrible": thus, "the gauntleted ghost of the Southern Seas" is called "the White Squall"; "human malice" chooses white as a "potent auxiliary" when "the desperate White Hoods of Ghent murder their bailiff in the market-place"; ghosts are white, death is white: it is because white is the color of "supernaturalism" that it "appals." There seems to be something no less than ontological about whiteness that loosens it from the contingent power of ordinary feelings: "in his other moods, symbolize whatever grand or glorious thing he will by whiteness, no man can deny that in its profoundest idealized significance it calls up a peculiar apparition to the soul." ⟨. . .⟩

As white is the color of the dreadful, it might also be called a boring color. Despite its containment of all tonal possibilities, it has itself no variety. Suggesting "muteness and universality," it escapes time; yet to make it speak to us, Ishmael has catalogued its manifestations at almost tedious length and duration, adducing the most varied creatures and events of the earth, air, and water until there seems little possibility of escape from his elemental piling up of examples; until, that is, the frightening stellar prospect of immense voids and a cold landscape of snow suggest not a perceivable order but a perceivable chaos: darkness visible rather than light: atheism, not the presence of God. The preceding examples from the realms of earth, air, and water become in the end subsumed under "the great principle of light" itself, a light which then floods the universe, isolating in retrospect each elemental instance so that everything in existence is suddenly stripped of its false colors and revealed in its elementally boring whiteness; and with the whiteness of dread characterizing all animate and inanimate nature, "the palsied universe lies before us like a leper."

Here, the emotion that constitutes white makes vibrantly visible as a presence the nothingness with which all existence is secretly sickened. Ishmael in this chapter has writ large the "supernatural hand" of his childhood; he has given it visibility and extension, if not form.

—Paul Brodtkorb, *Ishmael's White World: a Phenomenological Reading of* Moby Dick (New Haven: Yale University Press, 1965), pp. 115–16, 119

❖

ROBERT ZOELLNER ON AHAB'S WHALE AND ISHMAEL'S
WHALE

[Robert Zoellner (b. 1926), formerly a professor of
English at Colorado State University, has written *The
Salt-Sea Mastodon* (1973), a study of *Moby-Dick* from
which the following extract is taken. Here, Zoellner
argues that Melville makes use of two versions of Leviathan, one conceived by Ahab and the other by Ishmael.]

Among the Yankee simplicities hidden beneath the convolute
surface of *Moby-Dick,* none is more fundamental than the fact
that the novel incorporates two versions of Leviathan. One is
Ahab's whale. The other is Ishmael's whale. To confound them,
to deal with the cetological data as if they constituted a homo-
geneous expository continuum, is to confound the meaning of
Melville's novel. *Moby-Dick*—and the criticism of it—will
remain little more than a fascinating hodge-podge of the
"higgledy-piggledy whale statements" until the reader distin-
guishes Ahab's *transcendental* whale from Ishmael's *naturalistic*
whale.

     Ahab's whale can be dealt with in brief compass. It is aston-
ishing to discover what a small portion of Ahab's speaking lines
are devoted to comment on Moby Dick, or even on whales in
general. Ahab has less to say about Leviathan than
Shakespeare's Mercutio has to say about Queen Mab. In the
quarter-deck scene, we learn only that Moby Dick is a "white-
headed whale with a wrinkled brow and a crooked jaw, . . .
with three holes punctured in his starboard fluke"; his back is
full of harpoons, he has a spout "like a whole shock of wheat,"
and he "fan-tails" when he swims. Ahab is also exasperatingly
minimal in explaining what the albino whale *means* to him. Of
the forty lines of his "little lower layer" discussion, only five
deal directly with Moby Dick. The world, he tells Starbuck, is an
"unreasoning" pasteboard mask, an opaque perceptual wall
behind which a "still reasoning thing" hides itself. "To me, the
white whale is that wall, shoved near to me . . . He tasks me;
he heaps me; I see in him outrageous strength, with an
inscrutable malice sinewing it. The inscrutable thing is chiefly
what I hate; and be the white whale agent, or be the white
whale principal, I will wreak that hate upon him."

In sum: Moby Dick is illimitably strong. Moby Dick is pervasively malicious. Moby Dick is inscrutably intelligent. Moby Dick is physically vulnerable, perceptually violable. Moby Dick, finally, has bitten off my leg. These five propositions, crudely simplistic as they are, cover virtually all that Ahab has to say about his arch-enemy in the 135 chapters of a very long novel.

Ishmael tries to fill the gaps in Ahab's perfunctory account of his motivations, but even Ishmael's garrulous tendencies are satisfied with a single paragraph. "Small reason was there to doubt," he begins, establishing the speculative nature of what follows,

> . . . that ever since that almost fatal encounter, Ahab had cherished a wild vindictiveness against the whale, all the more fell for that in his frantic morbidness he at last came to identify with him, not only all his bodily woes, but all his intellectual and spiritual exasperations. The White Whale swam before him as the monomaniac incarnation of all those malicious agencies which some deep men feel eating in them, till they are left living on with half a heart and half a lung. That intangible malignity which has been from the beginning; to whose dominion even the modern Christians ascribe one-half of the world; which the ancient Ophites of the east reverenced in their statue devil;— Ahab did not fall down and worship it like them, but deliriously transferring its idea to the abhorred white whale, he pitted himself, all mutilated, against it. All that maddens and torments; all that stirs up the lees of things; all truth with malice in it; all that cracks the sinews and cakes the brain; all the subtle demonisms of life and thought; all evil, to crazy Ahab, were visibly personified, and made practically assailable in Moby Dick. He piled upon the whale's white hump the sum of the general rage and hate felt by his whole race from Adam down; and then, as if his chest had been a mortar, he burst his hot heart's shell upon it.

Nevertheless, it would be a mistake to assume from all of this that Ahab's pursuit of the whale is similar to Ishmael's— conceptual, inquiring, broadly philosophical. It is not. It is as narrowly personal, as visceral, as the clenching of a fist. During that first, pre-literary encounter, Ahab, his three boats stove and splintered, "seizing the line-knife from his broken prow, had dashed at the whale, as an Arkansas duellist at his foe, blindly seeking with a six inch blade to reach the fathom-deep life of the whale." Professionally this is equivalent—the reader will forgive a somewhat strained analogy—to a matador's suddenly flinging aside his cape and kicking the bull squarely in the ribs on his next pass. Ahab's petulant gesture with his six-inch knife reduces his confrontation with Moby Dick to a raw power-equation, an equation unable to bear the loading of meaning which Ishmael, endlessly inferential, gives it in the hints of the "Moby Dick" chapter. Ahab translates *all* meanings of the whale into the unmodulated idiom of brute force and simple power. This is evident in his speech to the corpusants, which he sees as an appropriately trinitarian manifestation of what Moby Dick represents. He has called the dying whale a "trebly hooped and welded hip of power." He now addresses invisible cosmic deity in the same terms, as "speechless, place-less power." Love, he says, is deity's "lowest form." Deity's "highest" form is "mere supernatural power," the most charac-teristic expression of which is the grossly quantitative launch-ing of "navies of full-freighted worlds."

These launched flotillas of worlds, these endless galactic armadas, are redolent of post-Copernican man's exploding world-view, his dispiriting sense of incomprehensible stellar distances and illimitable cosmic voids. They furnish the terms which define Ahab's whale, and distinguish it from Ishmael's: gross size, gross power, gross mass. Alfred Kazin has remarked that "The greatest single metaphor in the book is bigness." This is an oversimplification if the novel belongs (as it does) to Ishmael, but for Ahab it says all that needs saying. The *Pequod's* Captain and his whale stand as the best expression in American literature of what might be called the *empirical bogey,* technological man's resentful awareness of the steady erosion in stature which he has suffered ever since Galileo ground his first lens and Newton evolved his first principle. The pre-literary Ahab may have been a "mighty pageant creature," but the aging and mutilated Ahab of *Moby-Dick,* fronting an empirically conceived cosmos, is simply and pathetically *puny.* The "Leviathanism" of the whale expresses that which for Ahab is *the* salient quality of both the cosmos he can see and the deity he cannot see: sheer, gross *size.*

—Robert Zoellner, *The Salt-Sea Mastodon: A Reading of* Moby-Dick (Berkeley: University of California Press, 1973), pp. 146–49

❖

JANE MUSHABAC ON SERMONS IN *MOBY-DICK*

[Jane Mushabac (b. 1944) is a former professor of English at Baruch College of the City University of New York. In this extract from *Melville's Humor: A Critical Study* (1981), Mushabac comments on the function of the many sermons in *Moby-Dick* on conveying the philosophical thrust of the novel, notably the chapter "The Honor and Glory of Whaling."]

Melville's achievement in *Moby-Dick* has to do less with the game of little interchanges than the game of long talk. The book is full of sermons, full of "the best contradictory authorities" giving us their spiels. We have Ishmael's to Queequeg on fasting and fanaticism, Ishmael's to Bildad and Peleg on the First Congregational Church, Father Mapple's to the whalemen, Stubb's to Pip, Stubb's to Fleece, Fleece's to the sharks, and—above all and beneath all—Ishmael's from start to finish on one whaling voyage with one Queequeg, one Ahab, one Moby Dick. The humor at the beginning fumbles, it would seem, because the book is not yet firmly at sea. It is not just that the water itself puts everything in a continually, reliably precarious state of rocking and motion, but that the water is also the territory that Melville has for his own. There was much land humor, and there were many sea stories, but a watery prose humor of old salts and oceangoing isolatoes Melville had to himself. Once at sea also, Ishmael may take a more comfortable working position, less at the center of the action than at the side, as narrator, observer, anatomist, stand-up philosopher. His whole action from then on can become the talk, as it should be. He will occasionally take part in action or talk about himself, but mostly what we have from "The Advocate" on is Ishmael as the schoolmaster with the full "boggy, soggy, squitchy picture" before him, the picture of ultimate fascination, importance, and drama.

In "The Advocate" Melville gets into the heart of his subject and sets up the novel as a prodigious long piece of talk about one of man's activities. Thereafter Ishmael never needs to hesitate to find something to describe or explain. He hardly need turn his head, from Starbuck to Stubb to Flask to Ahab, to the whale, to a system of whales, to the whale's fin to his blubber to his organ to his tail, from the sighting of the whale to the killing of him to the boiling of him to the carving of his teeth, from one gam to the next to the next. So much to talk about! In *Moby-Dick,* Ishmael gets excited about many things; he invokes many gods and kings, and gives us many visions of heaven. "This is Charing Cross; hear ye! good people all,—the Greenland whale is deposed,—the great sperm whale now reigneth." Or he invokes that "democratic dignity which, on all hands, radiates without end from God; Himself! The great God absolute! The centre and circumference of all democracy! His omnipresence, our divine equality!" Or he dreams up a vision of a heaven of angels each with his hand in a jar of spermacetti. But truly Ishmael's image of glory is being able to talk, and from "The Advocate" on, he may go on as long as he pleases. No wonder the whale is, according to one of Ishmael's final etymological flourishes, "the Macrocephalus of the Long Words." *Moby-Dick* is not only a tall tale, but a long story, by another macrocephalus (big head of the long words), by Ishmael himself. And finally, if one notices the quiet inanity of Ishmael's description of Starbuck as a "long earnest man," one begins to see that Ishmael knows we are all long, earnest men (unless we are short, stubby ones). We all seek to defend our-selves—or match wits with the universe—by going on as long as we can.

Chapter 82, "The Honor and Glory of Whaling," is central to the book. Here Ishmael typically takes impossible leaps of logic as if he were merely crossing the street. He conjures up for our pleasure the gallant Perseus, who in a fine and lovely act res-cues and marries a maid. He conjures up St. George and with a quietly dazzling verbal legerdemain makes over the "tutelary guardian of England" and his dragon into whaleman and whale. Of Hercules we are told, "At any rate the whale caught him, if he did not the whale. I claim him for one of our clan." And finally Vishnoo is brought gently and firmly into the fold. "If I claim the demi-god then, why not the prophet," Ishmael asks, moving quickly and naturally on to the gods themselves. "Perseus, St. George, Hercules, Jonah and Vishnoo! there's a member-roll for you!"

Ishmael takes such liberties in the procedures of his talk that the reader's response in part is like Queequeg's, as that benevolent cannibal sits counting by fifties the pages of the incomprehensible book in his lap, "a long-drawn gurgling whistle of astonishment." Ishmael, however, has explained of man what is true of himself: "Nothing dispirits and nothing seems worth while disputing. He bolts down all events, all creeds, and beliefs and persuasions, all things visible and invisible, never mind how knobby." If Ishmael entangles the reader in the crisscrossing harpoon lines of getting a grip on that elusive thing called reality, considering that the whale cannot be simply stared in the face because he has none, Ishmael will try anything and with consummate energy and infinite good graces. He will let himself get carried away with a redundancy of alliteration, exclamation, and allusion. He will tell one part of his book, as a set of Shakespearean soliloquies, one as a cetological catalogue, one as a visit to a tropical temple surrounded by fierce but indolent natives, and the book as a whole as an anatomy of the world on a ship of fools. He will let Stubb inculcate "the religion of rowing" amongst his men, Flask whip up his to an atheistical orgasmic fury, and he himself get caught up in the current of fifty different sects: Christian, cannibal, Moslem, Hindu, ancient Hebrew, pragmatic American, and more. Ishmael is the predecessor of Beckett's Lucky, but when Ishmael commands himself "Think!" he has let himself in knowingly, willingly, and even happily for the foolishness he will make of himself.

At the end of *Moby-Dick*, the chapters fall off to what we may call tragic relief. Finally all talk gives way to the death song at its core—as "The Hyena" chapter liberates the clean ghost with a quiet conscience sitting snuggly in the family vault, the clean ghost who is Ishmael at his best. Finally everyone dies except Ishmael who swims off with the sharks, padlocks on their mouths—and, in effect, on his. The book that begins by following funerals and ends with the death of a nation is from beginning to end a song about what it is like to have survived your own death.

—Jane Mushabac, *Melville's Humor: A Critical Study* (Hamden, CT: Archon Books, 1981), pp. 82–85

[Bainard Cowan is the editor of *Theorizing American Literature: Hegel, the Sign, and History* (1991) and the author of *Exiled Waters:* Moby-Dick *and the Crisis of Allegory* (1982), from which the following extract is taken. Here, Cowan studies the degree to which Melville's novel can be considered an allegory.]

The multiple approaches of *Moby-Dick* present a veritable anatomy of allegory. Melville was making an honest comment when he wrote Sophia Hawthorne "that the whole book was susceptible of an allegoric construction, & also that *parts* of it were." Our task is to take up the suggestions of the Hawthornes—though undoubtedly in ways far other than they could have conceived—to uncover both "the particular subordinate allegories" and "the part-&-parcel allegoricalness of the whole." The progressive phases of *Moby-Dick,* as I intend to show, perform an allegorical contemplation of the combined imperative and impossibility of reuniting those four great broken spheres of the modern world: the community; knowledge; the religious approach to God; history. The community is the first of these contemplative topics, and Ishmael discovers it by its inverse image, the exile.

In the first sentence of his narrative, Ishmael demonstrates the centrality of allegory to his existence as a literary character. He identifies himself only by allusion; from his reference one can gather that he is an outcast, an exile like the original Ishmael. The "real" name of the character behind this literary persona is never to be known; for the duration of his fictional existence he lives in exile in the linguistic sphere also, banished from a proper name and forced to adopt one which is his only allegorically. The sentence accomplishes a double turn on Christian typology, a turn that is the central transformation of Melville's allegory, for it both rejects and reincorporates the tradition in one stroke. The narrator identifies himself, the book's chief son and the only survivor of its events, with the son of Abraham who was cast out from the main line of sacred history, a first son made definitively second. The narrator's implied rejection of Isaac, the son who is first in sacred history, cannot be seen as the restoration of the first-born son to his supposedly natural primacy, thereby correcting an ancient error. It has to be rather a further displacement of primacy, an unseating of even the original "second" son (Isaac) from his chosen firstness. The reference to Ishmael thus implies an anti-typology, a second typology which in effect asserts the failure of the first. Is Melville's Ishmael, then, a kind of messiah of this subversive history? The original Ishmael would therefore be a foreshadowing *figura* calling for later fulfillment. The paradoxical fulfillment of this already emptied figure, a figure of absence, would have to be a savior who returns and reappropriates without ever losing his quality of exile and secondariness. The somewhat ironic and arbitrary way he designates himself, of course ("call me," not "I am"), has clear precedent: "Art thou the king of the Jews?" "Thou sayest it."

The tradition of primacy, by contrast, clearly belongs to Ahab, a character with the expansiveness, the command and will of Abraham as well as of the perverse king for whom he is named. But that primacy is easily dispensed with in any revisionary history, which has its good as well as its bad uses. Not only did the dogs lick his blood when he lay dead, as the naïve Ishmael duly notes, but this imagery is incorporated interestingly into Psalm 68, a postexilic hymn wherein Ahab is no longer mentioned by name but is implicitly identified with "the enemy": "The Lord said, I will bring again from Bashan, I will bring my people again from the depths of the sea: That thy foot may be dipped in the blood of thine enemies, and the tongue of thy dogs in the same" (Ps. 68: 22–23). It is more than coincidence that the chosen people returning from exile are said to be brought back "from the depths of the sea." Ishmael specifically locates the place of his narrative as "in those for ever exiled waters." One should not lose sight of the fact that Ishmael is in the position, in *Moby-Dick,* of being the revisionary historian.

—Bainard Cowan, *Exiled Waters:* Moby-Dick *and the Crisis of Allegory* (Baton Rouge: Louisiana State University Press, 1982), pp. 69–71

[James Duban (b. 1951) is a professor of English at the
University of Texas. In this extract from *Melville's Major
Fiction* (1983), Duban traces the parallel between whal-
ing and early American expansionism.]

The exact source, if any, of Melville's parallel between whaling
and expansionism, is, then, less important than the currency of
an idea that provides ample precedent for Ishmael's Prentiss-
like decree that Nantucket whalers have "overrun and conquered that watery world like so many Alexanders; parcelling
out among them the Atlantic, Pacific, and Indian oceans. . . .
Let America add Mexico to Texas, and pile Cuba upon Canada;
. . . two thirds of this terraqueous globe are the Nantucketer's.
For the sea is his; he owns it, as Emperors own empires." Here,
though, Ishmael exhibits enthusiasm of the sort that led the
Democratic Review to advise that "we may . . . be taking a
great deal for granted, in discussing the consequences of
extending our territorial limits further to the westward than the
boundaries of Texas, and to be unmindful of Mrs. Glass's
instructions in cooking a fish—first catch it." Suggestive for its
related political emphasis is an article in the *American Whig
Review* titled "Our Adventures in Search of a Cat Fish—with
. . . Directions how Not to Cook One when Caught." Catching
and cooking Texas was not all that difficult; but barbecuing
Mexico in its aftermath proved more exhausting: "Waste not
your precious time in taking cats, but *if* taken, dream not of
barbecuing them, but return them unsigned to the stream, and
so shall a great waste of time and patience be spared."

Melville's Ahab stands to learn much the same lesson insofar
as his career echoes that of the biblical King Ahab, whose crim-
inality in stealing Naboth's Vineyard (1 Kings 21) was, as Alan
Heimert shows, often cited in the nineteenth century to
denounce American expansionism in the Southwest.
"Arguments . . . addressed to our national cupidity and pride,"
warned one congressman debating the annexation of Texas,
"are the arguments with which Ahab reconciled to himself the
seizing of Naboth's Vineyard." Granted, the seemingly unrelat-
ed exasperation of losing a limb instigates the mischief of

Melville's Ahab. Melville, however, may have known how President Polk legitimized America's claims upon Texas by arguing that the Louisiana Purchase (1803) had given the United States absolute title to this land but that John Quincy Adams had foolishly "dismembered" the territory from the Union by ceding it to Spain as part of the Florida Treaty of 1819. Polk, therefore, often spoke less in terms of "annexation" than he did of "reannexation." Several U.S. senators even supported a resolution stating that "the country dismembered from the United States by the treaty of 1819 . . . OUGHT TO BE reunited to the United States." But in a rebuttal that possibly imbues with political overtones Ahab's vow to "dismember my dismemberer," Senator Thomas Hart Benton presented a lengthy review of the Texas issue, finally lauding the prudence of Andrew Jackson, who, "in seeking to recover the dismembered part of our own country . . . did not undertake to dismember the empire of a neighbor." And Melville may well have consulted the 1844 volume of the *Congressional Globe* that includes this passage, for it also contains an account of the stump speech in which Melville's brother, Gansevoort, coined the name "Young Hickory" for James K. Polk.

The expansionist nature of Ahab's quest also gives added significance to both "the sleeplessness of his vow" and to the fact that "even when wearied nature seemed demanding repose he would not seek that repose in his hammock." Ahab either paces the deck, "always wakeful" and mindful of his purpose, or he reclines at his charts with his head thrown back, as if he were reading the telltale, which, suspended from the ceiling, helps guide him to Moby-Dick. As Starbuck says, "[S]leeping in this gale, still thou steadfastly eyest thy purpose." Ahab's, in short, is an "unsleeping, ever-pacing thought," which finds an analog in the *Foreign Quarterly Review*'s criticism of both the "restless and reckless race" of American pioneers and "the American passion for going a-head, and keeping in perpetual motion." To this charge the New York *Herald* responded, insisting that Europe was merely intimidated by America's crusade to widen the area of liberty: "[I]t is this very 'restlessness' that alarms the despotisms of the ancient world—a 'restlessness' to which steam, the railroad, the electric telegraph . . . give such vastly increased impetus

and power. . . . " And Ahab's restlessness approaches this precise variety of continentalism: "The path to my fixed purpose is
laid with iron nails."

—James Duban, *Melville's Major Fiction: Politics, Theology, and Imagination* (DeKalb: Northern Illinois University Press, 1983), pp. 87–89

FRANK G. NOVAK, JR., ON MELVILLE'S USE OF BEAUTY AND TERROR

[Frank G. Novak, Jr., is a professor of humanities at
Pepperdine University. In this extract, Novak explores a
recurring pattern of opposition between beauty and
terror in *Moby-Dick*.]

As the *Pequod* enters the cruising grounds where she will
eventually encounter Moby Dick, a typhoon suddenly disrupts
the beauty and calm of "these resplendent Japanese seas." The
typhoon, Ishmael says, "will sometimes burst from out that
cloudless sky, like an exploding bomb upon a dazed and
sleepy town." Yet this phenomenon of unexpected terror suddenly erupting amidst peaceful beauty is not unusual: indeed,
as Ishmael observes, it commonly occurs in nature: "Warmest
climes but nurse the cruelest fangs: the tiger of Bengal crouch-
es in the spiced groves of ceaseless verdure. Skies the most
effulgent but basket the deadliest thunders: gorgeous Cuba
knows tornadoes that never swept tame northern lands."

This passage exemplifies a motif, a symbolic and thematic
pattern, which pervades *Moby-Dick*. This recurrent motif con-
sists of binary opposition between beauty and terror. In the
basic form of the motif, the appearance of beauty deceptively
conceals the terror which inevitably lurks beneath the surface.
The binary opposition of beauty and terror comprises the basic
symbolic structure and thematic intent of many descriptive passages and, in a broader sense, sustains a dialectical tension
which informs the entire novel. The beauty-terror dichotomy
appears in a variety of combinations; it is often a contrast
between physical appearances such as cats and tigers, days

and nights, the ocean's surfaces and depths, male and female. These physical opposites frequently possess a metaphysical significance by symbolizing the difference between such concepts as thought and emotion, inner realities and outward appearances, truth and illusion. The novel is, of course, replete with dual oppositions—good-evil, order-chaos, Christian-pagan, and so forth. Such symbolic and thematic tensions can be generally stated in terms of the opposition between beauty and terror; in other words, many of the forces or qualities which exist in binary opposition can be subsumed under the terror-beauty paradigm. Underlying many individual passages describing natural scenes as well as the overall symbolic structure, the beauty-terror opposition is the pervasive, the most consistently developed binary contrast in the novel. The contrast developed by this motif produces an effect, a tension which animates many of the novel's descriptive and symbolic passages: the more beautiful the scene or image, the more ominous and malevolent is the terror associated with it.

As a pervasive symbolic structure, the beauty-terror opposition is a fundamental form of what Charles Feidelson calls the novel's "primal patterns of conflict." Starbuck's tendency to discern "inward presentiments" in "outward portents" generally describes the way the universe is perceived in the book. This view also suggests a method of interpreting the images of binary opposition. Describing the dangers of waging war against the whale, Ishmael speaks of "the interlinked terrors and wonders of God." This association of terror with wonder, Starbuck's "inward presentiment" ironically signified by the "outward portent," resonates powerfully throughout the novel. In "A Bower in the Arsacides," for example, the pattern is developed in terms of the intimate juxtaposition of life and death; as the vines covered the skeleton of the whale, "Life folded Death; Death trellised Life; the grim god wived with youthful Life, and begat him curly-headed glories." Ishmael's description of the whale contains the same sort of contrast: "the graceful repose of the line, as it silently serpentines about the oarsmen before being brought into actual play . . . carries more of true terror than any other aspect of this dangerous affair." Whalemen, he contends, routinely encounter "virgin wonders and terrors." And the fact that "the incorruption of this most fragrant ambergris should be found in the heart of such decay" is typical of the many connected opposites one encounters at sea. These contrasts are at the heart of a basic symbolic and thematic pattern: the dual motif, the binary opposition of beauty and terror. Not incidentally do the passages which describe this startling but natural association of beauty and terror rank among the most poetic and powerful in the novel, containing rich, highly suggestive imagery and a sense of dramatic tension evoked by the contrast. The tension produced by the contrast charges these passages with a high level of poetic energy.

The beauty-terror antithesis which appears so frequently in *Moby-Dick* is adumbrated in Melville's review "Hawthorne and His Mosses." Here Melville asserts that the mind which possesses greatness and genius not only perceives the delightful, beautiful surfaces of life but also grapples with the terrors of existence which lie beneath; a recognition of life's beauty and joy must be accompanied by an awareness of what he calls the "power of blackness." The writer of genius possesses a highly developed sense of "humor and love," yet these sunny qualities must be complemented by "a great, deep intellect, which drops down into the universe like a plummet." Melville describes what he sees as the characteristic juxtaposition of beauty and terror, happiness and despair, joy and suffering manifest in Hawthorne's stories. In terms of both image and idea, several passages in the review presage what becomes a recurrent pattern in *Moby-Dick*: Melville notes the familiar "Indian-summer sunlight on the hither side of Hawthorne's soul," yet he emphasizes the other side which "is shrouded in blackness." One should not be deceived by superficial appearances in Hawthorne, he says, for though one "may be witched by his sunlight . . . there is the blackness of darkness beyond." This basic dichotomy of a dark, terrifying underside beneath the deceptive surface of beauty and mildness appears again and again in *Moby-Dick*, especially in descriptions of natural phenomena. Melville recognized this polarity in Hawthorne, a symbolic pattern reflecting a tragic sense of life, and incorporated a similar binary structure into *Moby-Dick*.

—Frank G. Novak, Jr., " 'Warmest Climes But Nurse the Cruellest Fangs': The Metaphysics of Beauty and Terror in *Moby-Dick*," *Studies in the Novel* 15, No. 4 (Winter 1983) : 332–34

WILLIAM B. DILLINGHAM ON ISHMAEL AS A SURVIVOR

[William B. Dillingham (b. 1930) is a former professor of English at Emory University and the author of *Frank Norris: Instinct and Art* (1969), *An Artist in the Rigging: The Early Work of Herman Melville* (1972), and *Melville's Later Novels* (1986), from which the following extract is taken. Here, Dillingham finds that the overriding tragedy of *Moby-Dick* is somewhat mitigated by Ishmael's survival at the end.]

To say that *Moby-Dick* is a novel of survival ⟨. . .⟩ is not to say that it is some kind of tribute to the human spirit. It is not a story of man's ultimate and complete victory over the forces that would destroy him. It could not stand as a triumphant illustration of William Faulkner's uplifting declaration in his Nobel Prize acceptance speech that "man will not merely endure: he will prevail . . . because he has a soul, a spirit capable of compassion and sacrifice and endurance." Ishmael's survival is not meant to inspire hope for the human race but *awe,* awe that this particular person, complex, moody, and brilliant, could live through the wreck of the *Pequod* and its aftermath or through—to put it another way—the tidal-wave challenges that threaten his body and mind.

Yet, live through them he does, always with the instinct of survival working within him. It is not as if he loves life so well that he cannot tolerate the thought of giving it up. Quite the contrary. He is melancholy, even subject to deep depression (the "hypos" he calls this state of mind); he feels keenly the "damp, drizzly November" in his soul; and he even contemplates suicide. At times he, like the author who created him, believes temporarily that he has become reconciled to his own "annihilation." But like Melville, Ishmael always takes steps to avoid it. His going to sea, he says at the very beginning of the story, is for him an act of survival. It is his "substitute for pistol and ball." Cato may throw "himself upon his sword," but Ishmael "quietly take[s] to the ship." His doing so is not another form of suicide but an act of self-preservation taken in such a desperate moment as when others might kill themselves. Throughout, his narrative is punctuated both with indirect admonitions and with warnings about multifold dangers to survival. Narcissus, he says, plunged into the fountain and was drowned. "Heed it well," he warns Pantheistic visionaries, lest they "drop through the transparent air into the summer sea." Later he cautions: "Look not long into the face of the fire, O man! Never dream with thy hand on the helm! Turn not thy back to the compass." Nearly all these warnings grow out of Ishmael's own narrow escapes, after which he is moved to advise others about surviving.

Death and destruction are almost constantly on Ishmael's mind. Where others would look at harpoons and lances as tools of the trade of whaling, Ishmael sees them as implements of death. Whereas others would view the weapons of a heathen culture that decorate the walls of the Spouter Inn as fascinating curiosities, he shudders as he gazes at them and wonders "what monstrous cannibal and savage could ever have gone a death-harvesting with such a hacking, horrifying implement." The bartender, who stands in an area made to resemble the head of a right whale, seems to him to be in the "jaws of swift destruction." Such references to the dangers of whaling life serve to enhance the element of adventure in *Moby-Dick* and to create suspense and excitement about things to come, but there are so many of them and they occur so frequently and at times when an ordinary person (much less an ordinary whale-man) would not think of peril and death that they serve as well to reveal in Ishmael an unusual sensitivity that is the comple-ment to his survival instinct. He senses one kind of peril or another wherever he looks, and he states clearly the extent of these threats and his intentions with regard to them when he says early in the novel, "It is quite as much as I can do to take care of myself." Though the immediate context is comedy, his cry when Queequeg first crawls into bed with him is a serious expression of an intuitive determination: "Save me!"

Ishmael, then, is a man with a highly sensitized, ever-alert, built-in danger-detector operating on the electric current of his survival instinct. The ending of *Moby-Dick* with its widespread destruction has the unmistakable ring of tragedy, it is true, and even the epilogue strikes a melancholy note in the way Ishmael describes his being fished from the sea: *"It was the devious-cruising Rachel, that in her retracing search after her missing children, only found another orphan."* The sense of rootlessness and loneliness in Ishmael is strong here, but reverberating as well through the epilogue are the powerful words: *"One did survive the wreck."* It is important thematically that *only* Ishmael and, sadly, no one else lives through the ordeal, but it is equally significant that Ishmael *does* survive. An orphan, on the one hand, is a sad spectacle because mother and father are dead and the child has been left alone, but on the other hand, and on the positive side, an orphan is a survivor, the one who gets through the accident, the epidemic, the war, or other perils, alive. Ishmael's epilogue, therefore, should not be read merely as the final melancholy note in a tragic symphony but also as his quiet but proud announcement of survival with dignity.

Ishmael is thus by nature a survivor, sharing traits of character with other survivors of the world who live through physical trials and the aftermaths and who hold themselves together (if sometimes barely) through psychological crises. What some of these shared traits are can be seen in modern studies of the survivor as a type. In the twentieth century a considerable body of literature has emerged that deals with the survivors of Soviet work camps, Nazi death camps, and even lunatic asylums. Sociologists, historians, and psychologists who have devoted themselves to this subject have concluded that in the broadest terms survivors appear to have in common three traits. Though Melville of course could have no knowledge of Siberian political prisoners or of the Holocaust ordeal, he had enough insight into human nature and into himself to depict in the survivor of *Moby-Dick* these same precise qualities.

—William B. Dillingham, *Melville's Later Novels* (Athens: University of Georgia Press, 1986), pp. 133–37

ROBERT K. MARTIN ON *MOBY-DICK* AND SLAVERY

[Robert K. Martin (b. 1941) is a professor of English at the University of Montreal. He has written *The Homosexual Tradition in American Poetry* (1979) and *The Continuing Presence of Walt Whitman* (1992). In this extract from his book on Melville (1986), Martin shows that *Moby-Dick* presents a satire on slavery in its ironic contention that people can be regarded as property.]

The issue of slavery was important to all Americans of the mid-nineteenth century, but it took on special significance for Melville because of the role of his father-in-law, Judge Lemuel Shaw. Shaw's defense of segregated schooling, and his decision to return a fugitive slave to his master, made him part of the corrupt world Melville was attacking, although by indirection. The chapter on "Fast Fish and Loose Fish" has particular significance in this regard. For here Melville turned to the language of the law to show the ways in which a legal system would operate to uphold the values of property as against those of individual liberty. His analysis shows the connections between the legal status of women, slaves, and colonies, linking them all by his fishing metaphor that underlines the symbolic nature of the *Pequod* and its hunt. The conclusion of the chapter is a hilarious parody of the judicial quibbling that ignores every significant issue, followed by a series of contrasts that illustrate Melville's tendency toward the multiplication of tropes. For all ownership may ultimately be considered under the canopy of fishing law. A woman who is married is harpooned, hence a fast-fish: if she is married again, she is re-harpooned and now "that subsequent gentleman's property." As women are the property of their husbands, so are the conquered nations the property of the colonial powers, Ireland the fast-fish of Britain, or Texas the fast-fish of the United States (Melville's allusion to the conquest of Texas in the Mexican War). By these laws of property, we must imagine that a slave is a fast-fish, although if he escapes, should he not then be a loose-fish until chased down again? Melville's ironic questions are designed to bring forth the recognition that laws serve only to imprison men and that freedom is a rare achievement. By treating slaves and women as if they were property, that is, as if they were fish, Melville reveals the gap between codified law and morality.

—Robert K. Martin, *Hero, Captain, and Stranger: Male Friendship, Social Critique, and Literary Form in the Sea Novels of Herman Melville* (Chapel Hill: University of North Carolina Press, 1986), pp. 89–90

LEO BERSANI ON THE *PEQUOD* AS A METAPHOR FOR AMERICA

[Leo Bersani, a professor of French at the University of California at Berkeley, is a distinguished critic and author of *Marcel Proust: The Fictions of Life and Art* (1965), *A Future for Astyanax* (1976), *The Freudian Body: Psychoanalysis and Art* (1986), and other volumes. In this extract, Bersani ponders the degree to which the crew of the *Pequod* can be considered a metaphor for a racially and culturally diverse America.]

Is the *Pequod,* to the extent that it functions outside Ahab's domination, the image of an authentically democratic work society? Perhaps—but the workforce is constituted by a hybrid collection of exiles and outcasts. Not only does the biblical name by which the narrator invites the reader to address him in the novel's first line resonate such connotations; the latter aptly describe the crew of the *Pequod.* Ishmael's emphasis on all the countries and races represented on the ship invites us to see the crew as a kind of international fraternity of men united in harmonious and useful work. But there is an equally strong emphasis on the wild, untutored, asocial nature of the men in that fraternity. "They were nearly all Islanders in the Pequod, *Isolatoes* too, I call such, not acknowledging the common continent of men, but also each *Isolato* living on a separate continent of his own." It is, as Starbuck says, "a heathen crew . . . whelped somewhere by the sharkish sea," a crew, as Ishmael puts it, "chiefly made up of mongrel renegades, and castaways, and cannibals." Indeed whalers in general are "floating outlaws," manned by "unaccountable odds and ends of strange nations come up from the unknown nooks and ash-holes of the earth."

Ishmael himself must be thought of as belonging to that group; he is its expression. He is so casual in his dismissals of ordinary assumptions about social bonds that we may easily miss his readiness to reject the values of the land. "For my part," he announces in chapter one, "I abominate all honorable respectable toils, trials, and tribulations of every kind whatsoever." In context, this is playfully perverse hyperbole; but it also belongs to what amounts to a systematic rejection of the civilized ethics of a democratic and Christian land society.

71

Honorable respectable toils are abominated; the chapter on the Fast-Fish and Loose-Fish is a Swiftean mockery of legal systems in which rights to ownership are often identical to the brute force necessary to claim possession; and Christianity itself is implicitly dismissed in the comparison of images of physical "robustness" in art ("in everything imposingly beautiful, strength has much to do with the magic") to "the soft, curled hermaphroditical Italian pictures" of Christ, which "hint nothing of any power, but the mere negative, feminine one of submission and endurance, which on all hands it is conceded, form the peculiar practical virtues of his teachings." The *Pequod* is not, however, a reconstitution of politics, morality, or religious beliefs on some presumably more natural basis. Queequeg's religion is as unsatisfactory as Christianity, and Ishmael's infinite tolerance, far from being grounded in a faith where tolerance is preached as a virtue, merely expresses his unwillingness to be intolerant in the name of any faith whatsoever. Nor is Ishmael willing to swear allegiance to the *Pequod's* society of savages as a type of social organization. "I myself am a savage, owning to no allegiance but to the King of the Cannibals; and ready at any moment to rebel against him."

Is the *Pequod* an image of America? It is the settlement of America reenacted, but uncompromisingly radicalized. The "unaccountable odds and ends" from all over the world who ended up in America were of course not only castaways and cannibals; nor were they all, for that matter, unaccountable. But by insisting on the *Pequod's* nearly total break with the land and the past, Melville simultaneously evokes the origins of America as a house for exiles from everywhere and makes those origins absolute. That is, he evokes the possibility of exile as a wholly new beginning and brutally deprives it of the comforting notion of loss. There is no dream that has been frustrated, no second chance for forms of life imagined, but then blocked in their realization, somewhere else. The sea is wildness and anarchy; it opposes to both Ahab's despotism and the democratic vision a kind of social suicide. Thus Melville's novel dreams metaphorically of that absolute break with Europe which of course never took place, of a risky willingness to "come to America" with no social vision at all, with nothing but an anxious need to die to society and to history. Far from fulfilling a European dream, America would therefore have to be invented by those "thousands upon thousands of mortal men" who at first wanted nothing more than to flee from the land but who, having joined the crew of exiles and renegades from all over the hated world, now find themselves suspended in their dying and are obliged to redefine the social itself.

I have argued that, principally through Ahab, *Moby-Dick* dramatizes the oxymoronic impasse of democracy: the great man's despotism realizes the democratic dream of equality. But *Moby-Dick* also reinvents that politically infernal rhetoric as a political promise: it dreams a society owing nothing whatsoever to known social ideas. What this society after social death might actually be, we can say no more than Melville (or Ishmael) himself can. What can be said is only what has already been said, and Ishmael's way of coercing all that used speech into unimagined significances is to withdraw humorously from nearly all his propositions. He can say what he means only by refusing to mean what he says. America's history will take place in the space at once cluttered and blank where all imaginable social bonds have been simultaneously figured and dissolved. Melville's America is a historical meta-oxymoron: it defeats the defeating oxymoron of a democracy ruined by the fulfillment of its own promise by erasing all promises in order to make the wholly unauthorized promise of an absolutely new society.

—Leo Bersani, "Incomparable America," The Culture of Redemption (Cambridge, MA: Harvard University Press, 1990), pp. 148–50

JOHN B. WILLIAMS ON THE HISTORICAL BACKGROUND OF *MOBY-DICK*

[John B. Williams (b. 1941) is the author of *White Fire: The Influence of Emerson on Melville* (1991), from which the following extract is taken. Here, Williams examines the historical background of the sea adventures in *Moby-Dick*.]

The germ of *Moby-Dick*, as most readers know, is the true story of the ramming and sinking of the whaleship *Essex* from Nantucket by a sperm whale, which attacked the vessel twice on November 20, 1820, about two thousand miles west of the Galapagos Islands. Melville heard about this event in 1841 as a sailor aboard the whaler *Acushnet*, where he said it was occasionally a topic of forecastle conversation on the long voyage from Fairhaven around Cape Horn to the South Seas fishery. In July of that year, during a gam or visit on the high seas of the *Acushnet* with the whaler *Lima* from Nantucket, he met the sixteen-year-old son of Owen Chase, the first mate of the *Essex* who had written an account of the shipwreck and the ordeal of survival for the crew that followed. The youth, William Henry Chase, produced for Melville a printed copy of his father's narrative. Melville later reminisces: "The reading of this wondrous story upon the landless sea, and close to the very latitude of the shipwreck had a surprising effect on me."

Though Owen Chase's account is devoted largely to the harrowing experience of Captain George Pollard and his crew of the *Essex*, who drifted in open boats nearly 3000 miles for nearly three months and resorted to cannibalism before the last survivors were rescued, Melville's interest centered on the shipwreck; for this provides his materials for the climax of *Moby-Dick*. Of all Melville's novels to this point in his career, this is the only work in which the climax is both dramatic and preconceived. That Melville chose to brood over the story for nearly nine years, while composing five other novels, suggests that he was keeping it in reserve until he felt ready to work on it.

We can estimate the challenge of this episode to an impressionable mind disposed to perceive life in terms of symbols. In the beginning, Melville was attracted by the idea of the power and malice of the whale in purposely sinking a whaleship. To an inexperienced deckhand, the story must have combined qualities of myth and apocalyptic vision of the destruction of a fragile world similar to that of the *Acushnet*. Melville's sailor awareness of Nantucket as the principal whaling center for New England, with one hundred ships as opposed to about twenty in New Bedford and Fairhaven, must soon have directed his interest to probably the most important names associated with whaling on that island, and certainly the most colorful—Joseph Starbuck and Jared Coffin. They were wealthy merchants and ship owners, whose relatives were in many ways connected with the lore of whaling. A David Starbuck, for example, was killed by a whale in 1827; and an Owen Coffin, the cabin boy aboard the *Essex* and nephew of Captain Pollard, consented to let himself be eaten by members of the crew, so that they might survive the ordeal. But the names alone suggest the polarities of spiritual aspiration and morality that intrigued Melville. Had he visited Nantucket, although there is no evidence that he did before completing *Moby-Dick* in late summer of 1851, he would have found Captain Pollard's modest frame house, where he lived in retirement, across the street from the large brick Coffin House, an inn since 1845, and a few blocks away from the three adjoining Starbuck houses, also of brick. There within a short walk would be convenient reminders for a story on whaling: a survivor of the frightening attack on a ship and symbolic names associated with the precarious venture of hunting the sperm whale.

It is conceivable that in the early stages of his thinking Melville imagined a tragic contest between a star-bucking captain and a whale which turns his ship into a coffin. But his thought, nourished by his reading and especially by ideas from Emerson in 1849 and Hawthorne in 1850 and after, expanded into a complex symbolic drama of the mind at war with nature. In the novel, Melville ironically gives the name, Starbuck, to the prudent first mate aboard the doomed *Pequod* and sums up the idea of the defiant mind in Captain Ahab and the symbol of nature in the legendary white whale of the South Seas fishery. Melville uses the Coffin name in a variety of ways. In the opening paragraph of the novel, Ishmael finds himself standing before "coffin warehouses," such as would recall those of Jared Coffin as well as indicate Ishmael's depressed state of mind. Later, the proprietor of the Spouter Inn is Peter Coffin, whose function in the novel is to bring together Ishmael, the meditative outcast narrator, and Queequeg, the primitive harpooner who becomes Ishmael's bosom friend. Near the end, the *Pequod* fulfills the Parsee's prophesy and becomes a hearse, or carrier of coffins, as it sinks; and Ishmael floats to safety on a coffin made by Queequeg. We can sense in these details the play of Melville's imagination as he considers the problems of survival and annihilation in nature.

> —John B. Williams, *White Fire: The Influence of Emerson on Melville* (Long Beach: California State University Press, 1991), pp. 141–43

❖

JOHN BRYANT ON AHAB AS A TRICKSTER

[John Bryant (b. 1949) has written *Melville and Repose: The Rhetoric of Humor in the American Renaissance* (1993). In this extract from that work, Bryant studies Ahab as a traditional trickster figure, like Shakespeare's Falstaff.]

As a version of the dark-suited misanthrope and frontier trickster, Ahab enjoys a rich double heritage in satire. And given the novel's framed structure, we would expect Ahab to be the central brooding satirist whose antidemocratic attacks would be contained if not ameliorated by the genial Ishmael's framing cosmopolitan vision. It is a wonder that Ahab is not more laughable. Melville has deprived Ahab of the humanizing humors that would make his satire palatable: the benevolence of Goldsmith's Drybone or the sentiment of Kotzebue's "The Stranger." Overall, Ahab's satire is so fully attached to his "ontological heroics" that his politics (Machiavellian, monarchic, capitalistic) are merely a symptom of his egoism. In all, Ahab is the shell of a satirist; the cone of a nearly extinct volcano, erupting now and again upon the political scene, but not with any more specific satiric object in view than the demagogue in general or "man in the mass."

Mirroring his picturesque sensibility, Ishmael's politics are based on a Kantian and cosmopolitan synthesis of associative and dissociative instincts. While the soul may persist in "keep[ing] the open independence of her sea," it equally craves society. It is as fast as it is loose. Ahab's politics derive from a purely isolationist, not associative, ontology, and as a leader he ignores the responsibility of guiding the alienated crew toward cosmopolitan restraint. Melville's political goal is to reconcile these oppositions, to subsume the dissociative within the associative, and more specifically to bring egocentric leaders in line with the inevitable, cosmopolitan force of history.

It is a structural peculiarity of *Moby-Dick* that Ishmael and Queequeg, the two characters most capable of enacting a full cosmopolitan rebellion against Ahab's autocracy, are in fact removed from the action. The former's narratorial detachment and the latter's repose necessarily deprive them of this agency. Ishmael's genial desperation and sensual love for Queequeg are merely private discoveries that, while they symbolically prevail over Ahab, have no dramatic effect upon captain or crew. The cosmopolitan ideal is a universal religion that Ishmael keeps to himself. But this disempowerment of Ishmael and Queequeg makes comic sense, for if Ahab is to rediscover his associative instinct, his cosmopolitanism must grow logically out of his solipsism.

Melville's gambit in dramatizing the potential in Ahab for a cosmopolitical efflorescence is to let a set of fools act out for him a coalescence of humor and satire. Stubb and Pip are these displacements of Ahab's humor. Melville's model for this structure of displaced fools was Shakespeare, whose genial Falstaff and "mad" Edgar constitute comic visions that their "lords" are forced to keep at a distance. Melville's orchestration of Ahab's fools is connected to the plot, making this comic thread a crucial element in Ahab's dramaturgy. Moreover, Stubb and Pip represent, respectively, the failure and the redemption of geniality. Together, they conspire to bring Ahab back to a genial and cosmopolitan ideal and thereby promote Melville's politics of reconciliation. Thus Ahab's fools voice Melville's most prescient political statements concerning America, race, and national unity.

—John Bryant, *Melville and Repose: The Rhetoric of Humor in the American Renaissance* (New York: Oxford University Press, 1993), pp. 219–20

❖

Works by Herman Melville

Typee: A Peep at Polynesian Life. 1846. 2 vols.

Omoo: A Narrative of Adventures in the South Seas. 1847.

Mardi: And a Voyage Thither. 1849. 2 vols.

Redburn: His First Voyage: Being the Sailor-Boy Confessions and Reminiscences of the Son-of-a-Gentleman, in the Merchant Service. 1849.

White-Jacket; or, The World in a Man-of-War. 1850.

Moby-Dick; or, The Whale. 1851.

Pierre; or, The Ambiguities. 1852.

Israel Potter: His Fifty Years of Exile. 1855.

The Piazza Tales. 1856.

The Confidence-Man: His Masquerade. 1857.

Battle-Pieces and Aspects of the War. 1866.

Clarel: A Poem and Pilgrimage in the Holy Land. 1876. 2 vols.

John Marr and Other Sailors with Some Sea-Pieces. 1888.

Timoleon, etc. 1891.

Some Personal Letters and a Bibliography. Ed. Meade Minnigerode. 1922.

Works (Standard Edition). 1922–24. 16 vols.

The Apple-Tree and Other Sketches. Ed. Henry Chapin. 1922.

Journal Up the Straits: October 11, 1856–May 5, 1857. Ed. Raymond Weaver. 1935.

Collected Poems. Ed. Howard P. Vincent. 1947.

Complete Stories. Ed. Jay Leyda. 1949.

Journal of a Visit to London and the Continent 1849–1850.
Ed. Eleanor Melville Metcalf. 1948.

The Portable Melville. Ed. Jay Leyda. 1952.

Letters. Ed. Merrell R. Davis and William H. Gilman. 1960.

Writings (Northwestern-Newberry Edition). Ed. Harrison
Hayford et al. 1968–93. 15 vols. (to date).

At the Hostelry and Naples in the Time of Bomba. Ed. Gordon
Poole. 1989.

Works about
Herman Melville and
Moby-Dick

Adler, Joyce Sparer. *War in Melville's Imagination.* New York: New York University Press, 1981.

Baird, James. *Ishmael.* Baltimore: Johns Hopkins University Press, 1956.

Bloom, Harold, ed. *Ahab.* New York: Chelsea House, 1991.

———, ed. *Herman Melville's* Moby-Dick. New York: Chelsea House, 1986.

Boughn, Michael. "Eros and Identity in *Moby-Dick.*" *American Transcendental Quarterly* 1 (1987): 179–96.

Bowen, Merlin. *The Long Encounter: Self and Experience in the Writings of Herman Melville.* Chicago: University of Chicago Press, 1960.

Brodhead, Richard H., ed. *New Essays on* Moby-Dick. Cambridge: Cambridge University Press, 1986.

Canaday, Nicholas, Jr. *Melville and Authority.* Gainesville: University of Florida Press, 1968.

Dimock, Wai-Chee. *Empire for Liberty: Melville and the Poetics of Individualism.* Princeton: Princeton University Press, 1989.

Dryden, Edgar A. *Melville's Thematics of Form: The Great Art of Telling the Truth.* Baltimore: Johns Hopkins University Press, 1968.

Edinger, Edward A. *Melville's* Moby-Dick: *A Jungian Commentary.* New York: New Directions, 1978.

Finkelstein, Dorothee Metlitsky. *Melville's Orienda.* New Haven: Yale University Press, 1961.

Franklin, H. Bruce. *The Wake of the Gods: Melville's Mythology.* Stanford: Stanford University Press, 1963.

Fredericks, Nancy. *Melville's Art of Democracy.* Athens: University of Georgia Press, 1995.

Garner, Stanton. *The Civil War World of Herman Melville.* Lawrence: University Press of Kansas, 1993.

Grenberg, Bruce L. *Some Other World to Find: Quest and Negation in the Works of Herman Melville.* Urbana: University of Illinois Press, 1989.

Gretchko, John M. J. *Melvillean Loomings: Essays on Moby-Dick.* Cleveland: Falk & Bright, 1992.

Haberstroh, Charles J., Jr. *Melville and Male Identity.* Rutherford, NJ: Fairleigh Dickinson University Press, 1980.

Hamilton, William. *Reading* Moby-Dick *and Other Essays.* New York: Peter Lang, 1989.

Hayes, Kevin J., ed. *The Critical Response to Herman Melville's* Moby-Dick. Westport, CT: Greenwood Press, 1994.

Heimert, Alan. "*Moby-Dick* and American Political Symbolism." *American Quarterly* 15 (1963): 498–534.

Karcher, Carolyn L. *Shadow over the Promised Land: Slavery, Race, and Violence in Melville's America.* Baton Rouge: Louisiana State University Press, 1980.

Kaul, A. N. "Herman Melville: The New-World Voyageur." In Kaul's *The American Vision: Actual and Ideal Society in Nineteenth-Century Fiction.* Westport, CT: Greenwood Press, 1963, pp. 214–79.

Kirby, David. *Herman Melville.* New York: Continuum, 1993.

Lackey, Kris. " 'More Spiritual Terrors': The Bible and Gothic Imagination in *Moby-Dick.*" *South Atlantic Review* 52 (1987): 37–50.

Lebowitz, Alan. *Progress into Silence: A Study of Melville's Heroes.* Bloomington: Indiana University Press, 1970.

Leyda, Jay. *The Melville Log: A Documentary Life of Herman Melville 1819–1891.* New York: Harcourt, Brace, 1951.

McCarthy, Paul. *"The Twisted Mind": Madness in Herman Melville's Fiction.* Iowa City: University of Iowa Press, 1990.

McWilliams, John P., Jr. *Hawthorne, Melville, and the American Character: A Looking-Glass Business.* Cambridge: Cambridge University Press, 1984.

Markels, Julian. *Melville and the Politics of Identity: From King Lear to* Moby-Dick. Urbana: University of Illinois Press, 1993.

Pease, Donald E. "*Moby Dick* and the Cold War." In *The American Renaissance Reconsidered,* edited by Walter Benn and Donald E. Pease. Baltimore: Johns Hopkins University Press, 1985, pp. 113–31.

Percival, M. O. *A Reading of* Moby-Dick. Chicago: University of Chicago Press, 1950.

Person, Leland S., Jr. *Aesthetic Headaches: Women and a Masculine Poetics in Poe, Melville, and Hawthorne.* Athens: University of Georgia Press, 1988.

Pommer, Henry. *Milton and Melville.* Pittsburgh: University of Pittsburgh Press, 1950.

Pops, Martin Leonard. *The Melville Archetype.* Kent, OH: Kent State University Press, 1970.

Reeve, F. D. *The White Monk: An Essay on Dostoevsky and Melville.* Nashville: Vanderbilt University Press, 1989.

Reno, Janet. *Ishmael Alone Survived.* Lewisburg, PA: Bucknell University Press, 1990.

Rogin, Michael Paul. *Subversive Genealogy: The Politics and Art of Herman Melville.* New York: Knopf, 1983.

Rosenberry, Edward H. *Melville.* London: Routledge & Kegan Paul, 1979.

Samson, John. *White Lies: Melville's Narratives of Facts.* Ithaca, NY: Cornell University Press, 1989.

Schirmeister, Pamela. *The Consolations of Space: The Place of Romance in Hawthorne, Melville, and James.* Stanford: Stanford University Press, 1990.

Sealts, Merton K., Jr. *Melville's Reading.* Columbia: University of South Carolina Press, 1988.

Short, Bryan C. *Cast by Means of Figures: Herman Melville's Rhetorical Development.* Amherst: University of Massachusetts Press, 1992.

Stern, Milton R. *The Fine Hammered Steel of Herman Melville.* Urbana: University of Illinois Press, 1968.

Suchoff, David. *Critical Theory and the Novel: Mass Society and Cultural Criticism in Dickens, Melville, and Kafka.* Madison: University of Wisconsin Press, 1994.

Tolchin, Neal L. *Mourning, Gender, and Creativity in the Art of Herman Melville.* New Haven: Yale University Press, 1988.

Vincent, Howard P. *The Trying-Out of* Moby-Dick. Boston: Houghton Mifflin, 1949.

Weigman, Robyn. "Melville's Geography of Gender." *American Literary History* 1 (1989): 735–53.

Wright, Nathalia. *Melville's Use of the Bible.* Durham, NC: Duke University Press, 1949.

Young, Philip. *The Private Melville.* University Park: Pennsylvania State University Press, 1993.

Index of
Themes and Ideas